THE BENEFITS OF LOOKING UP

PARTNERS & SPADE

Photos taken on our iPhones August 2008 through July 2009

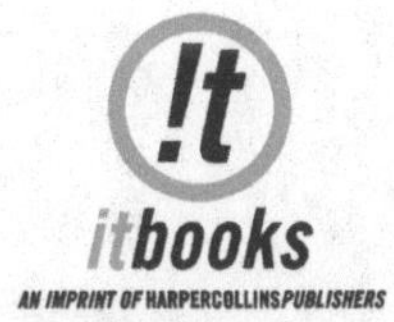

itbooks

For information, address HarperCollins Publishers,
10 East 53rd Street, New York, NY 10022.

HarperCollins books may be purchased for educational, business, or sales promotional use. For information, please write: Special Markets Department, HarperCollins Publishers, 10 East 53rd Street, New York, NY 10022.

FIRST EDITION

Designed by Partners & Spade

ISBN: 978-0-06-190166-9

09 10 11 12 13 10 9 8 7 6 5 4 3 2 1

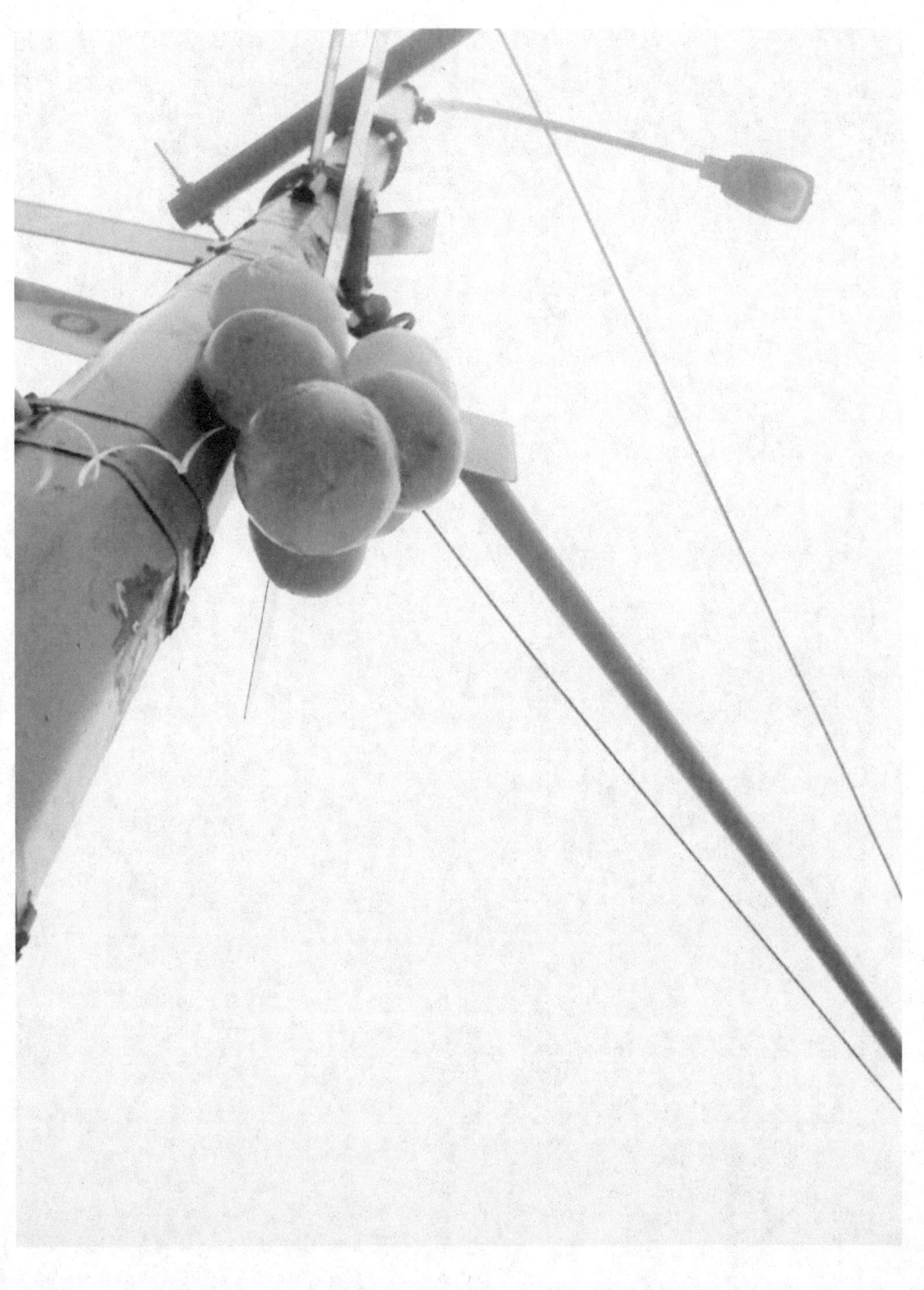

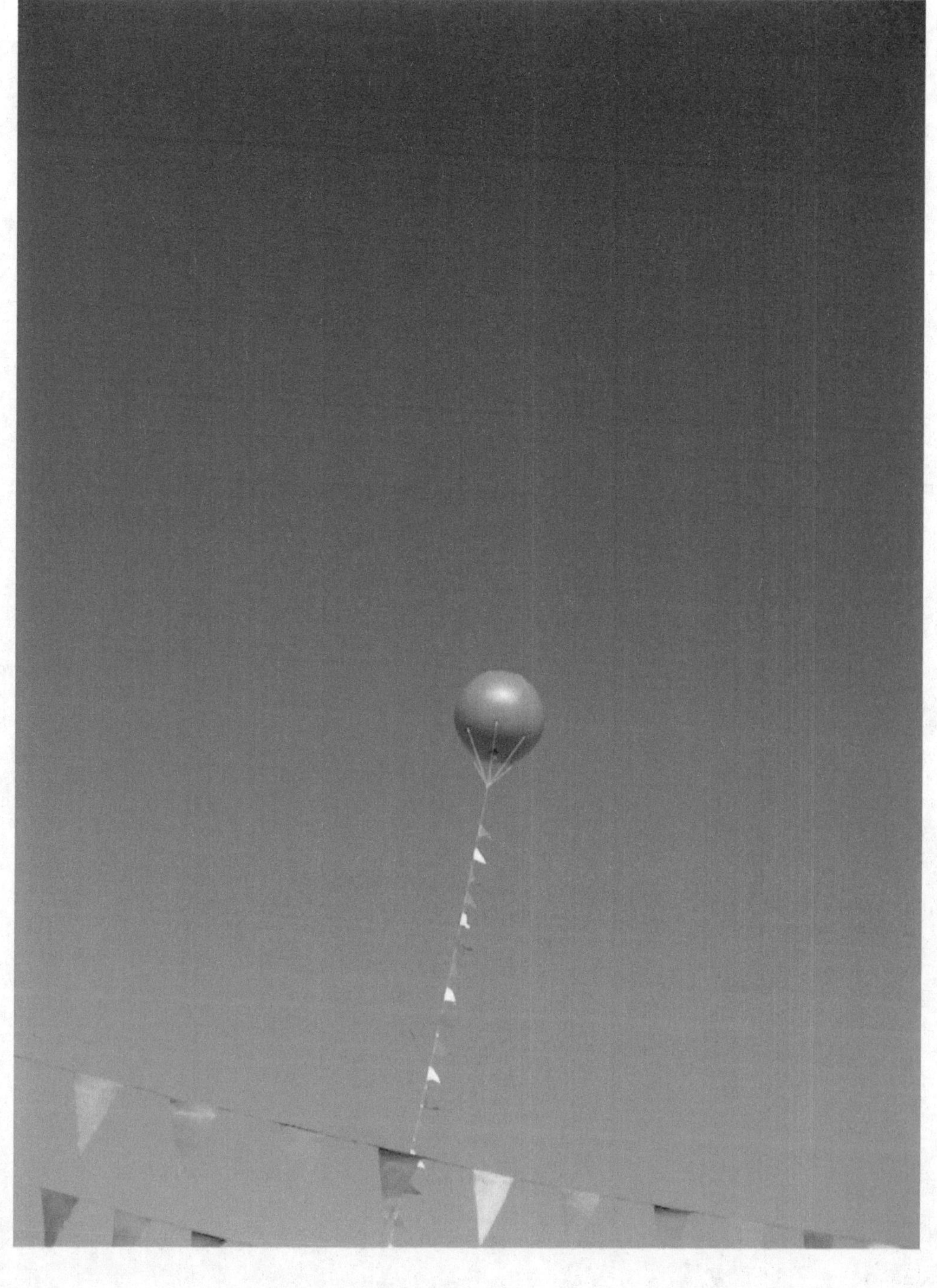

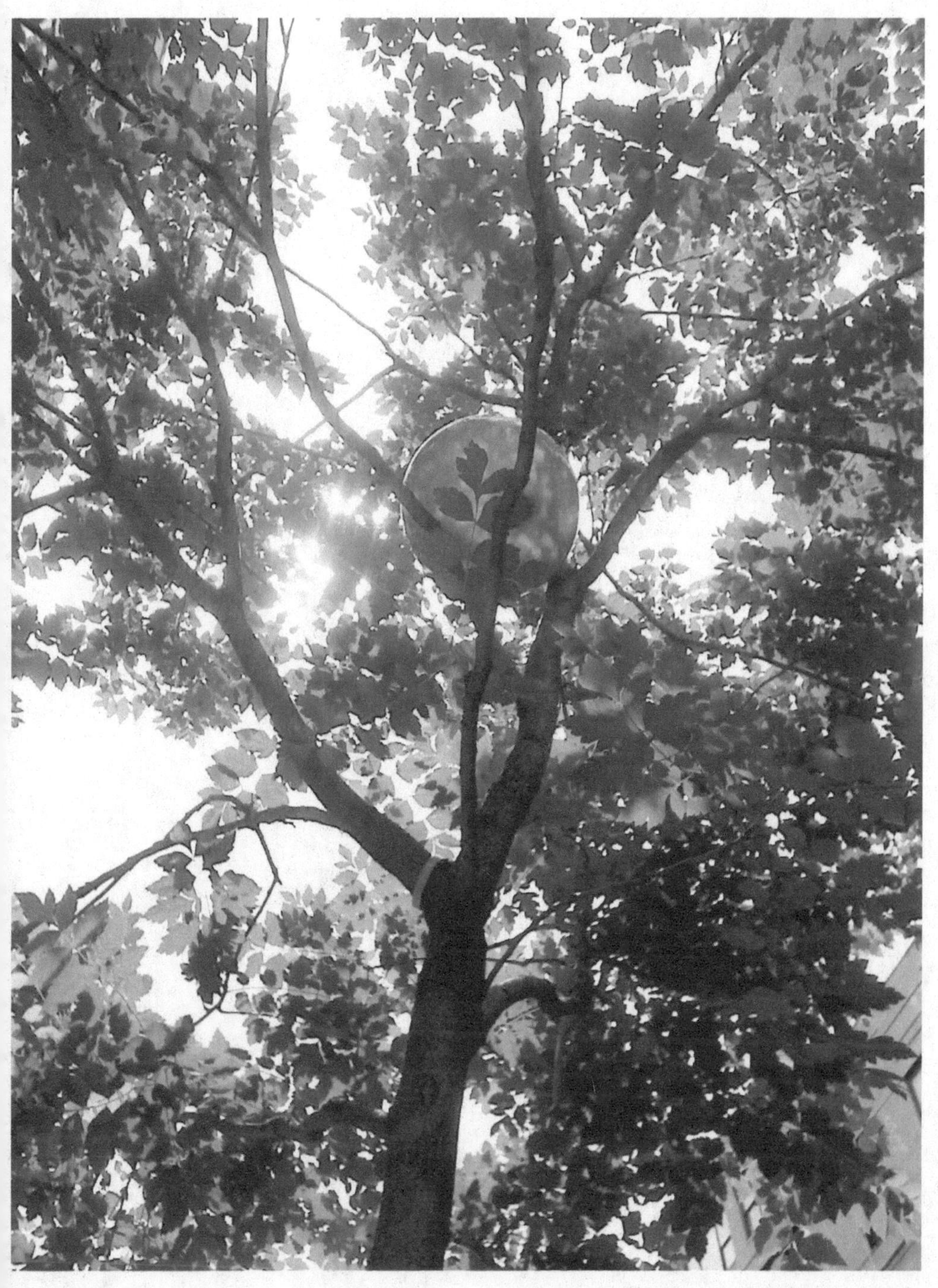

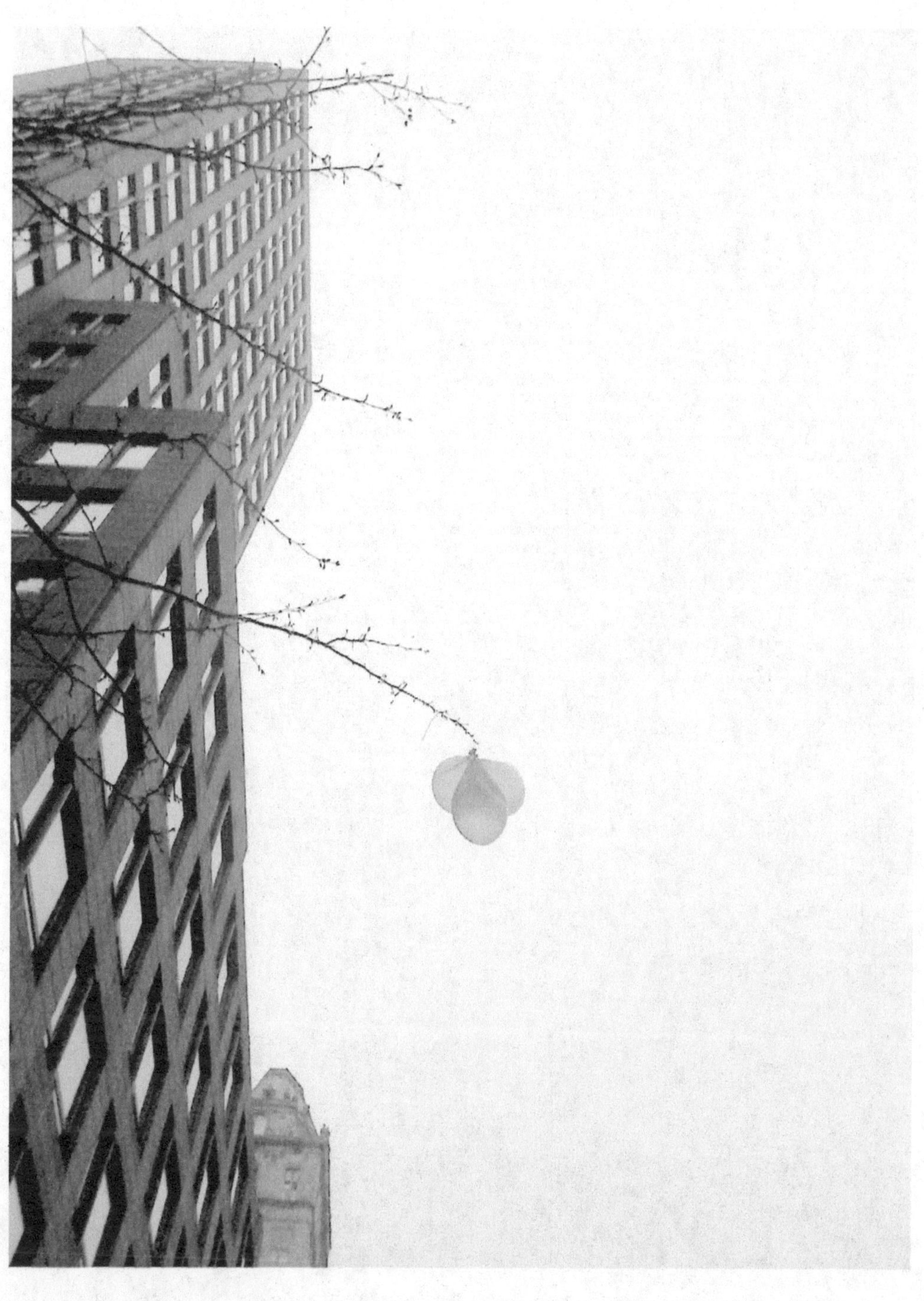

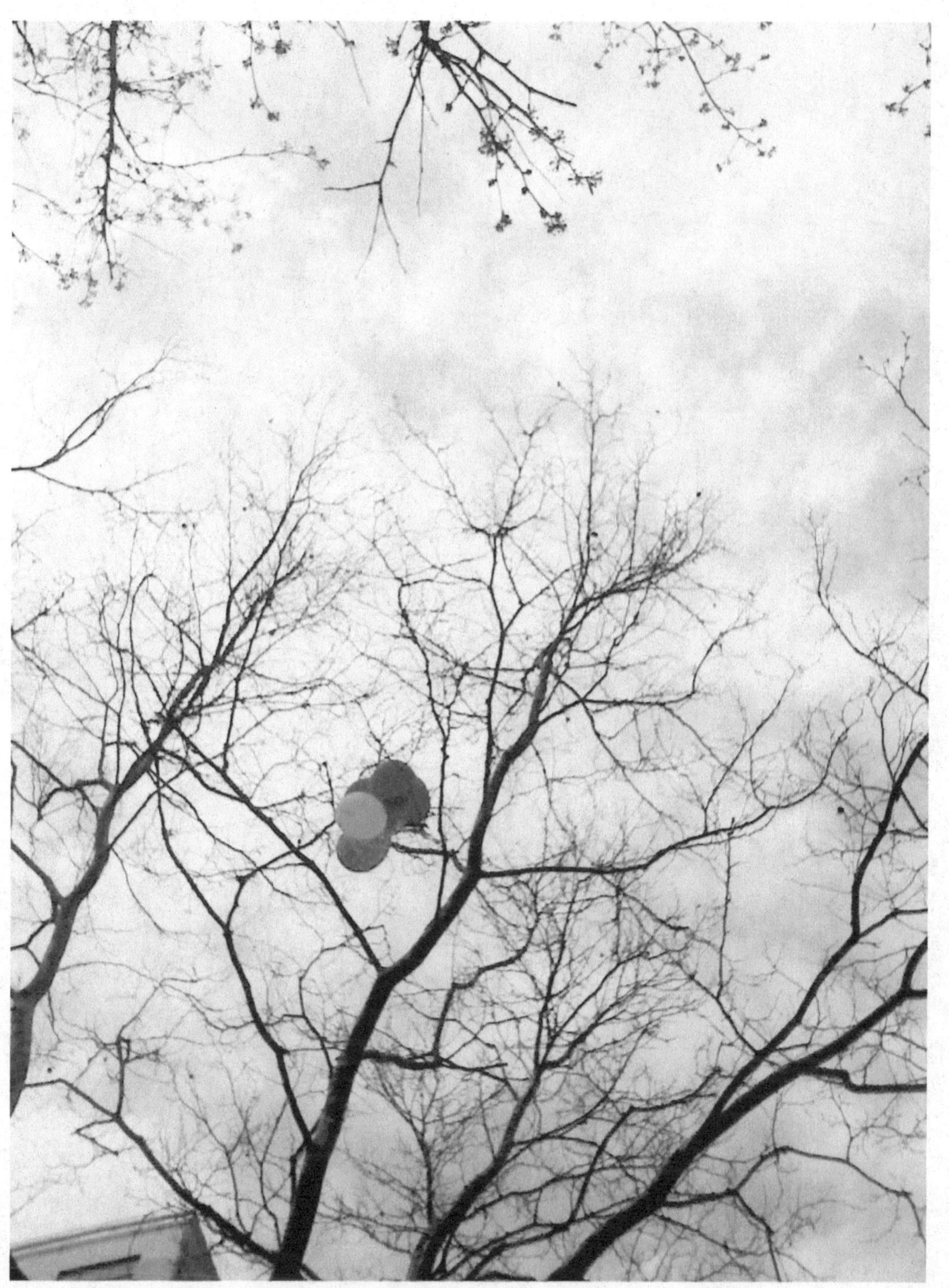

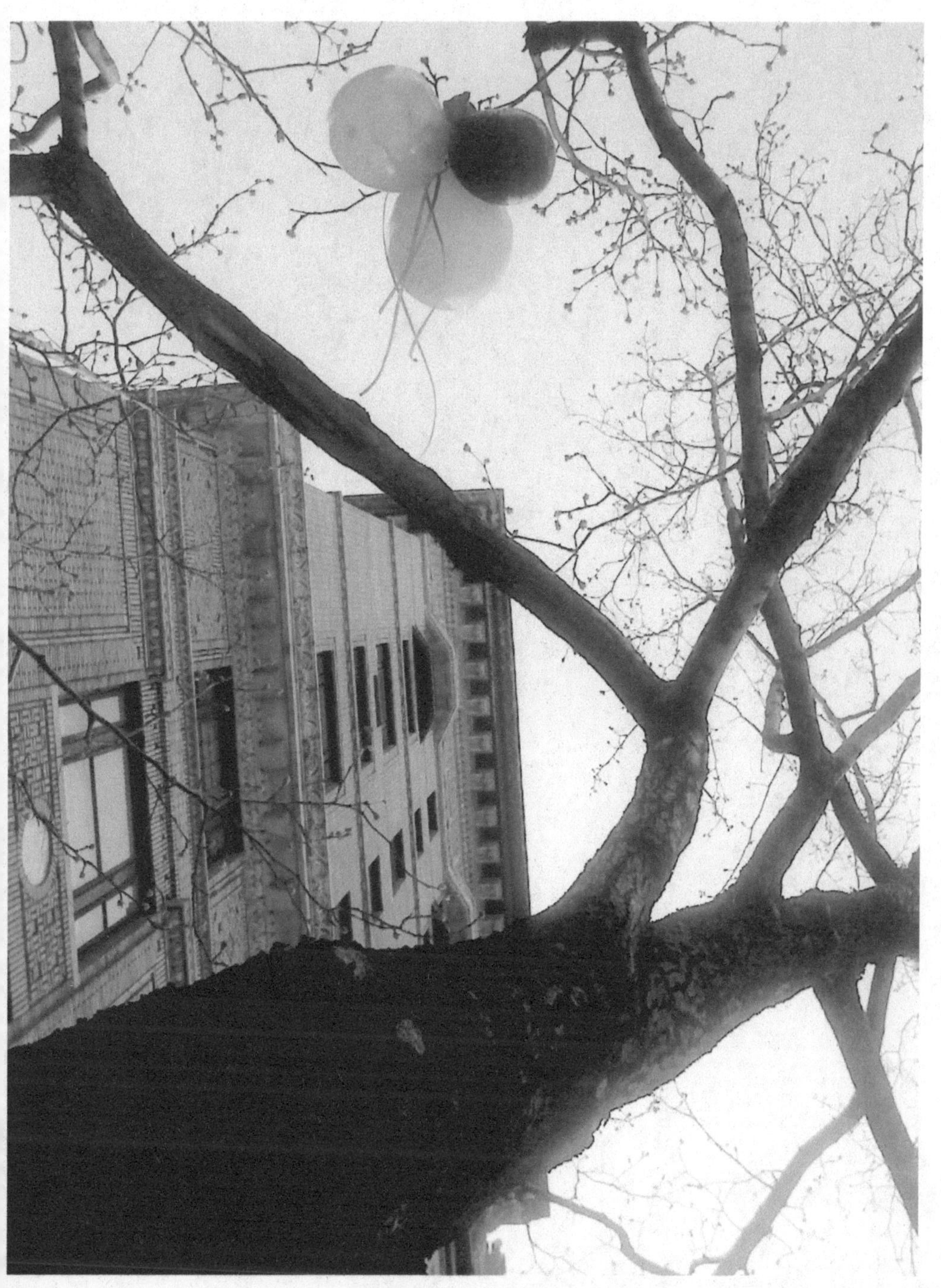

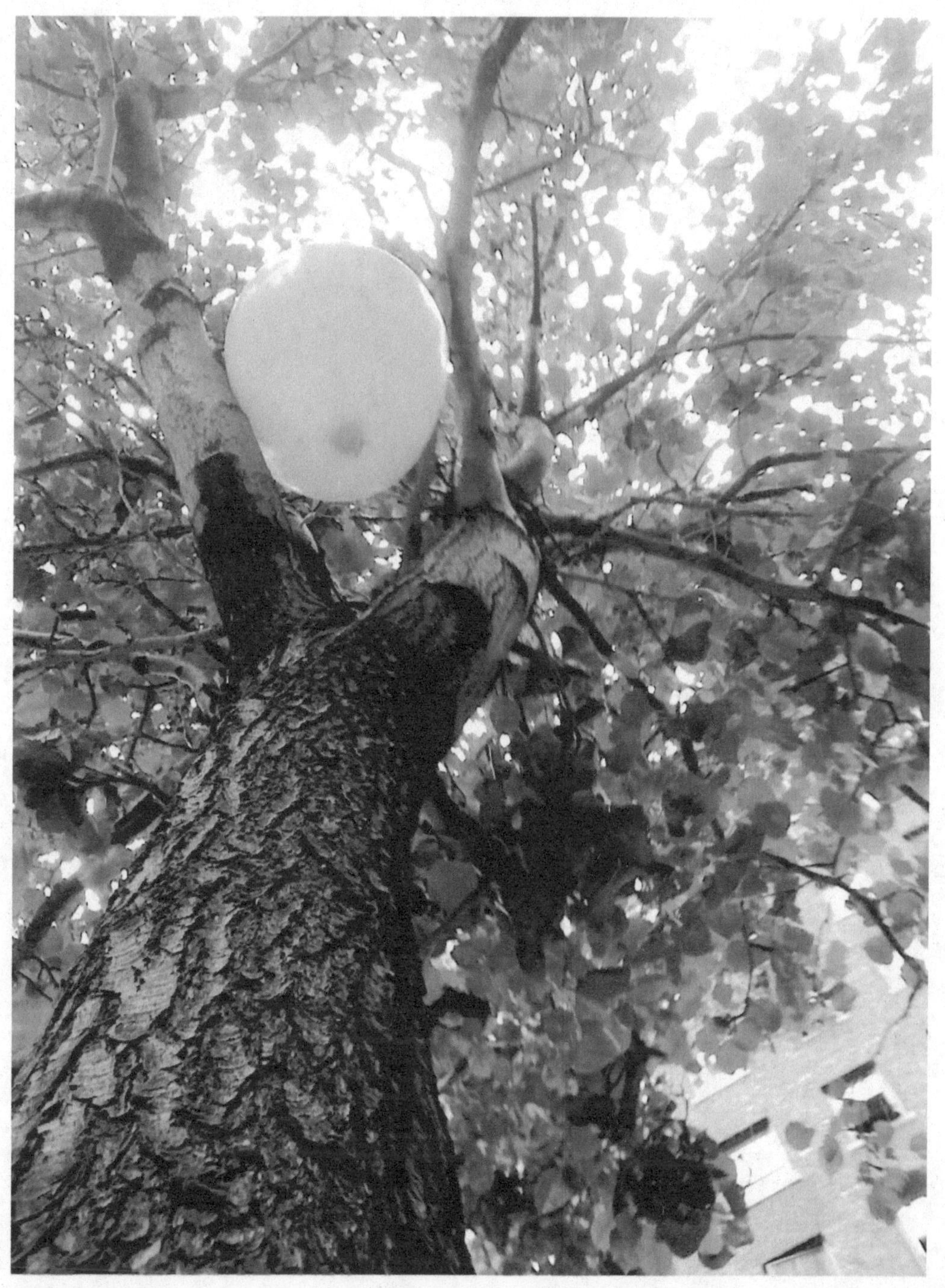

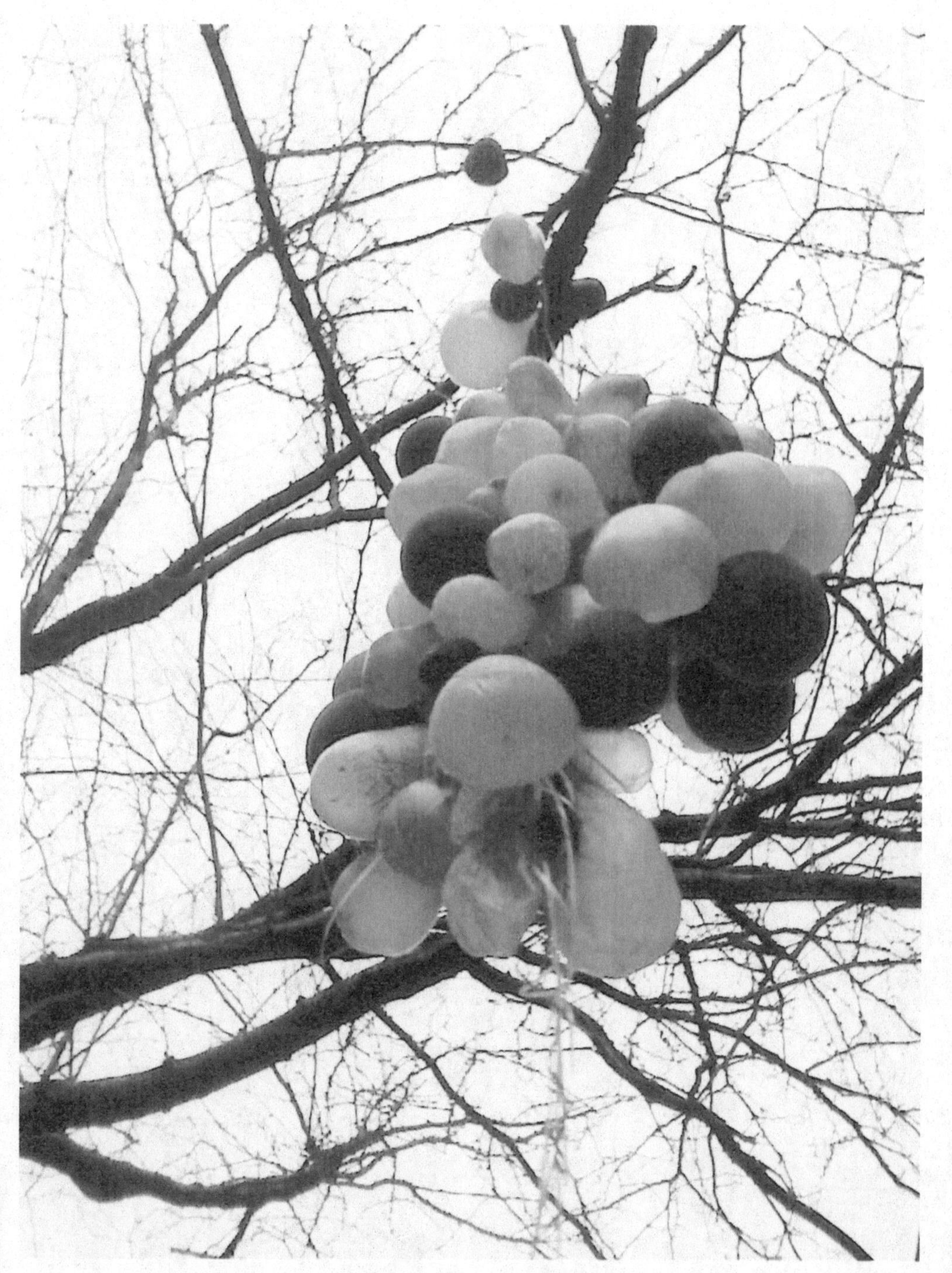

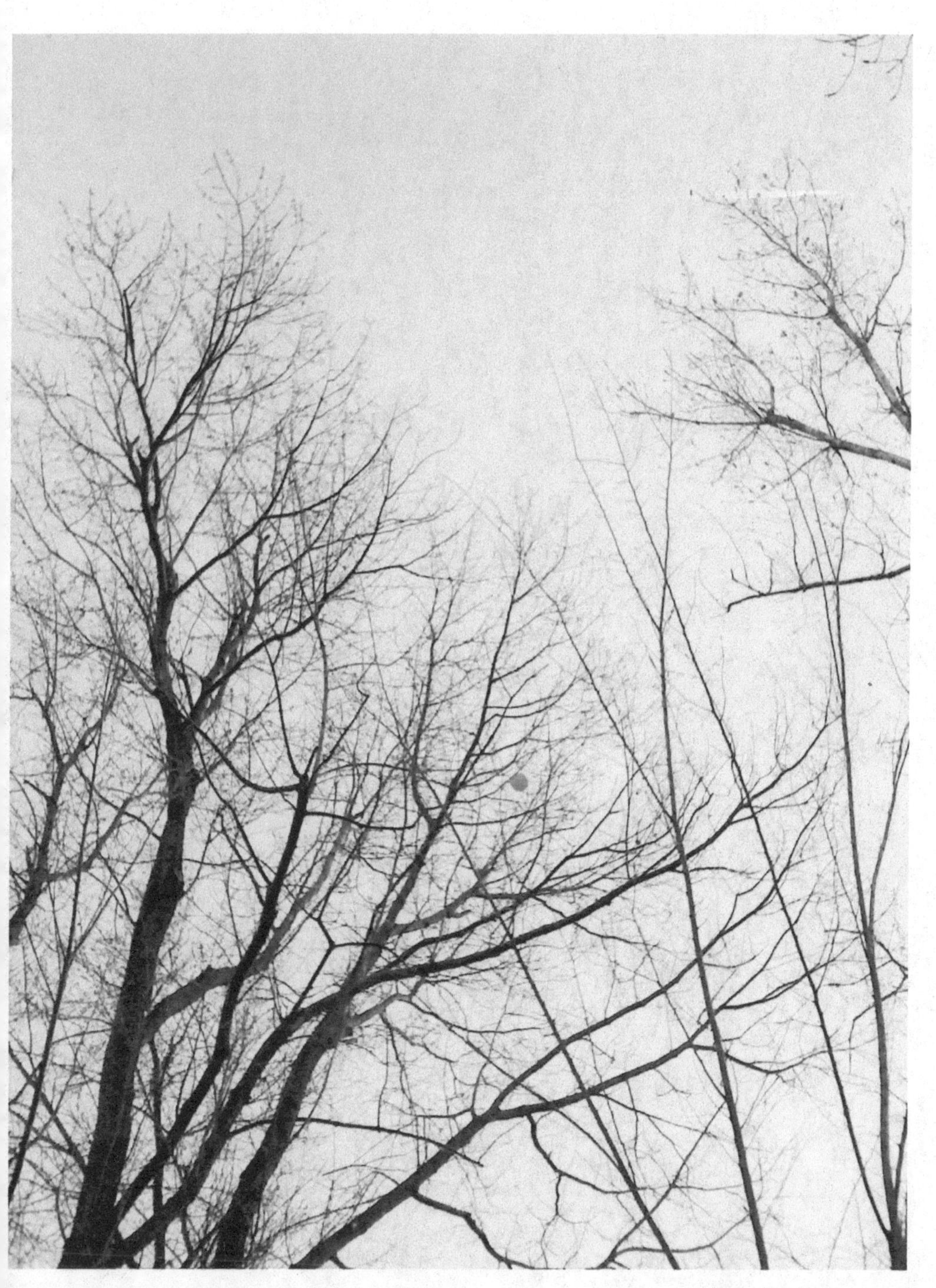

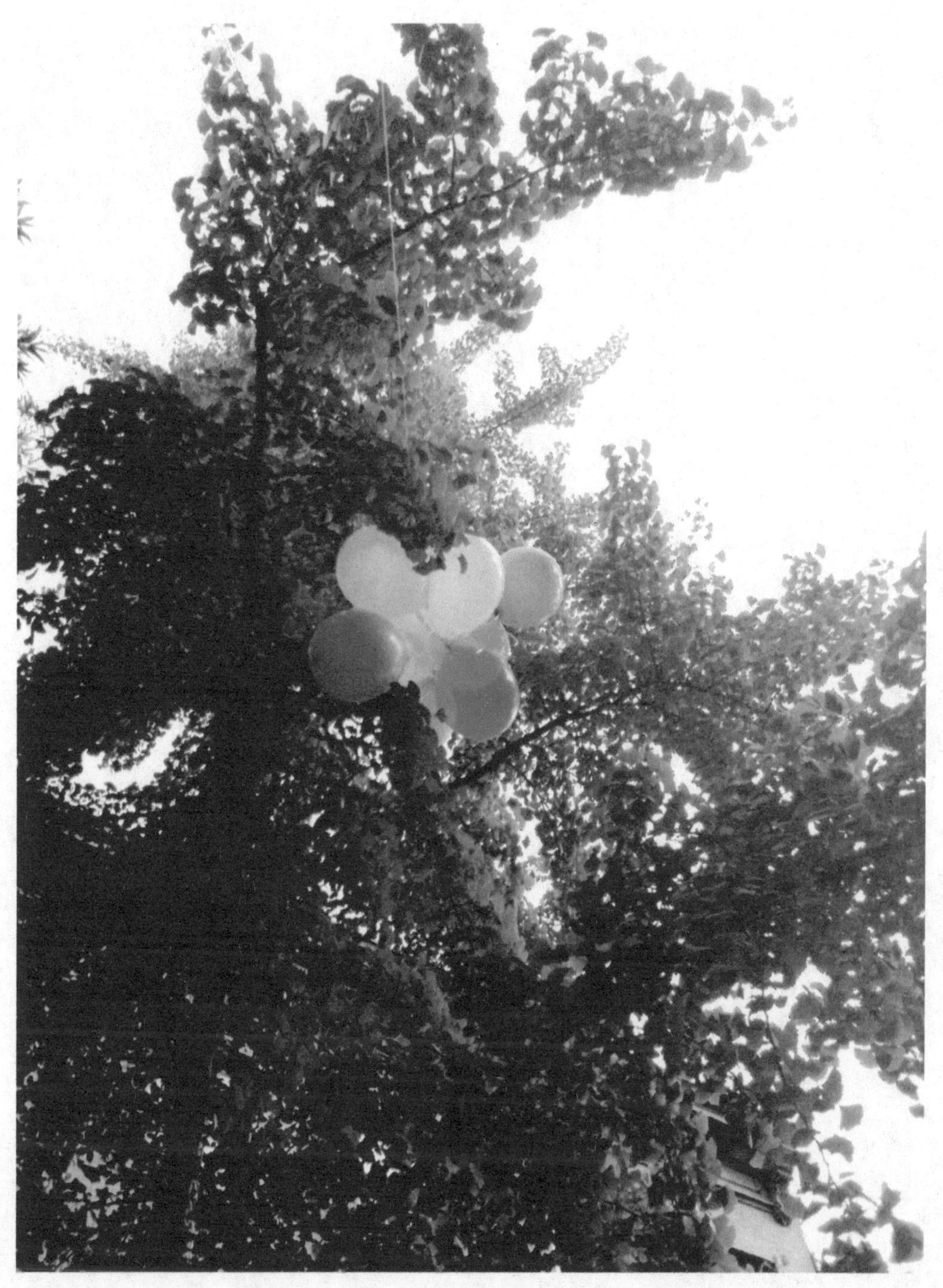

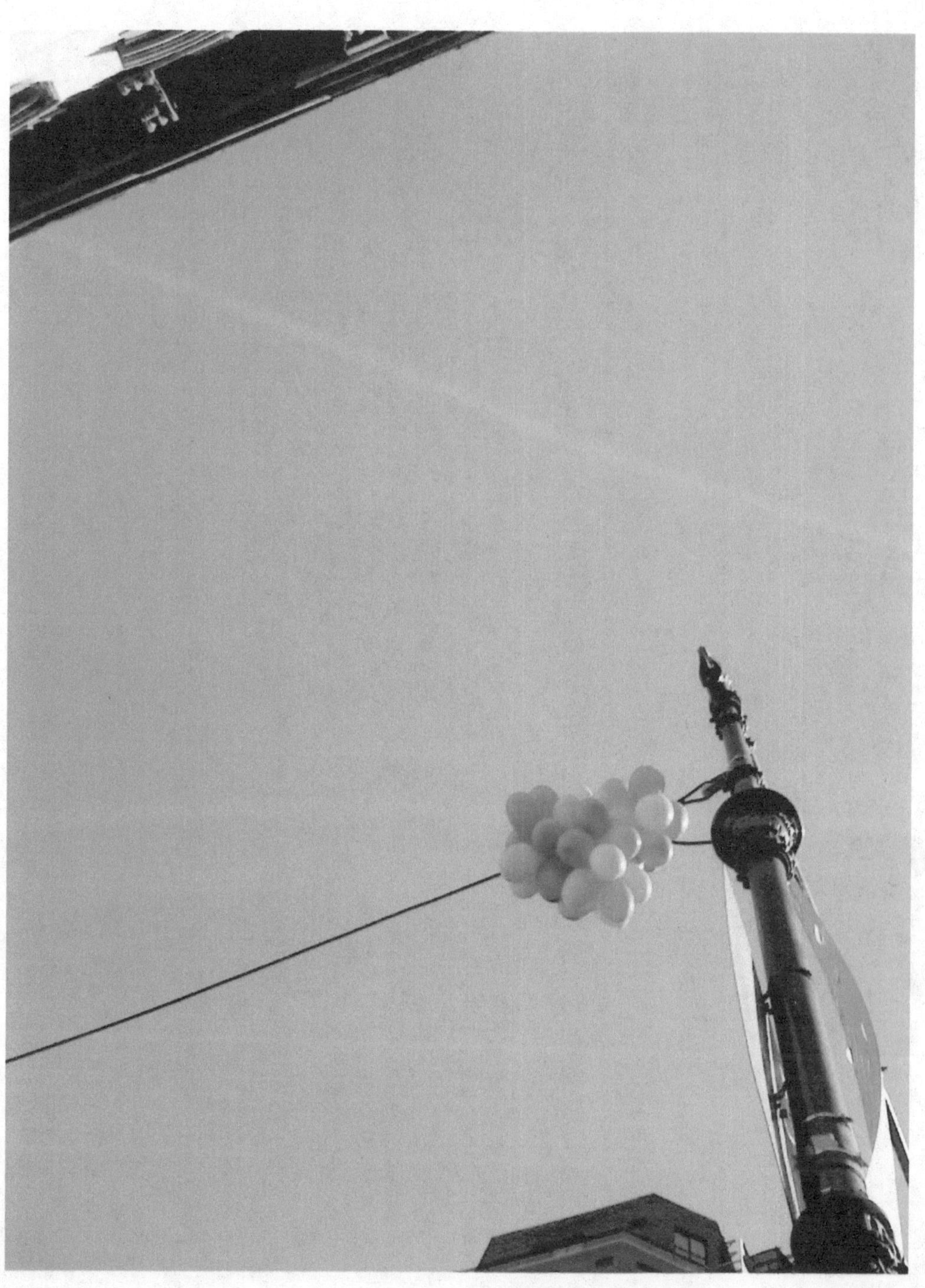

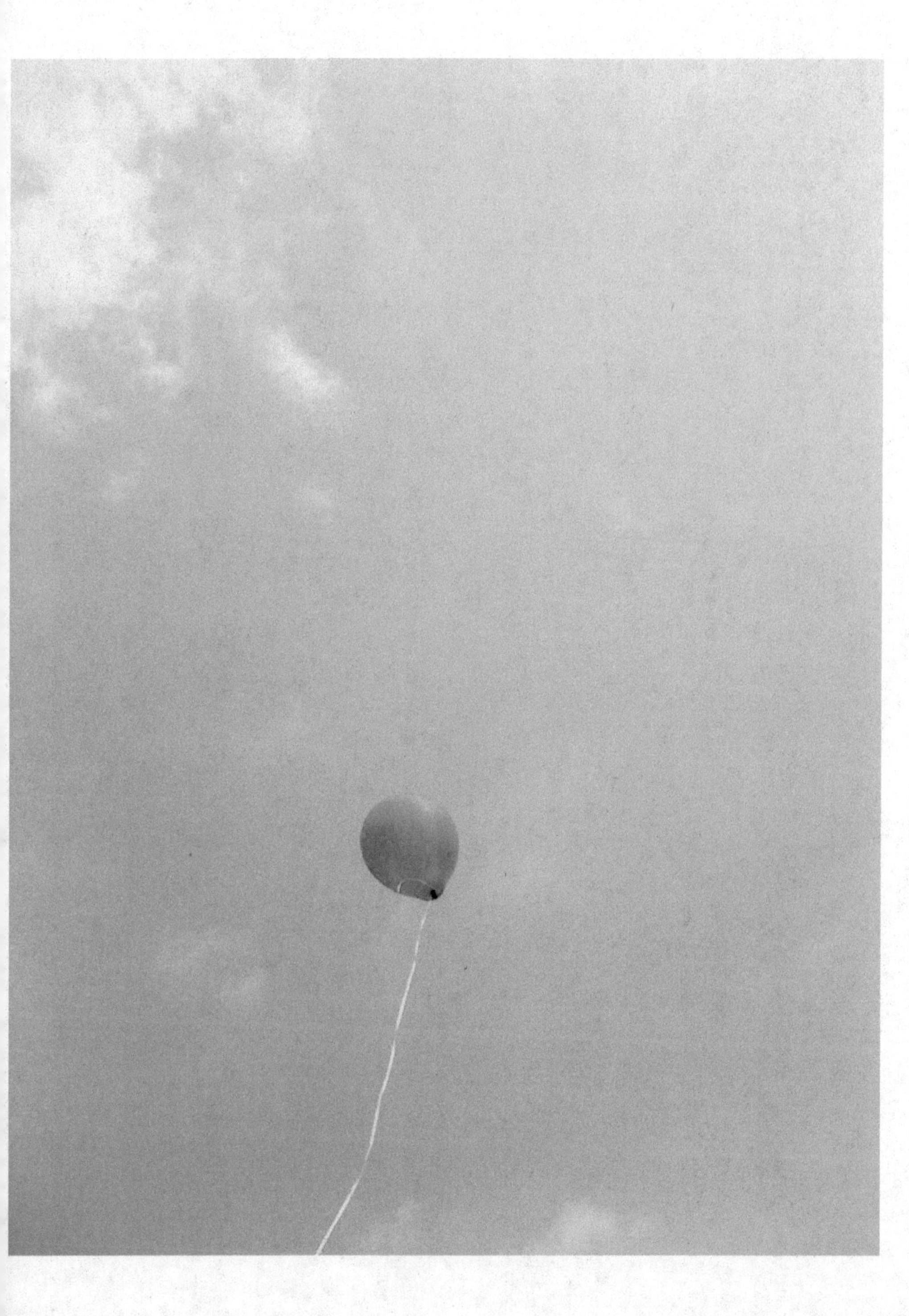

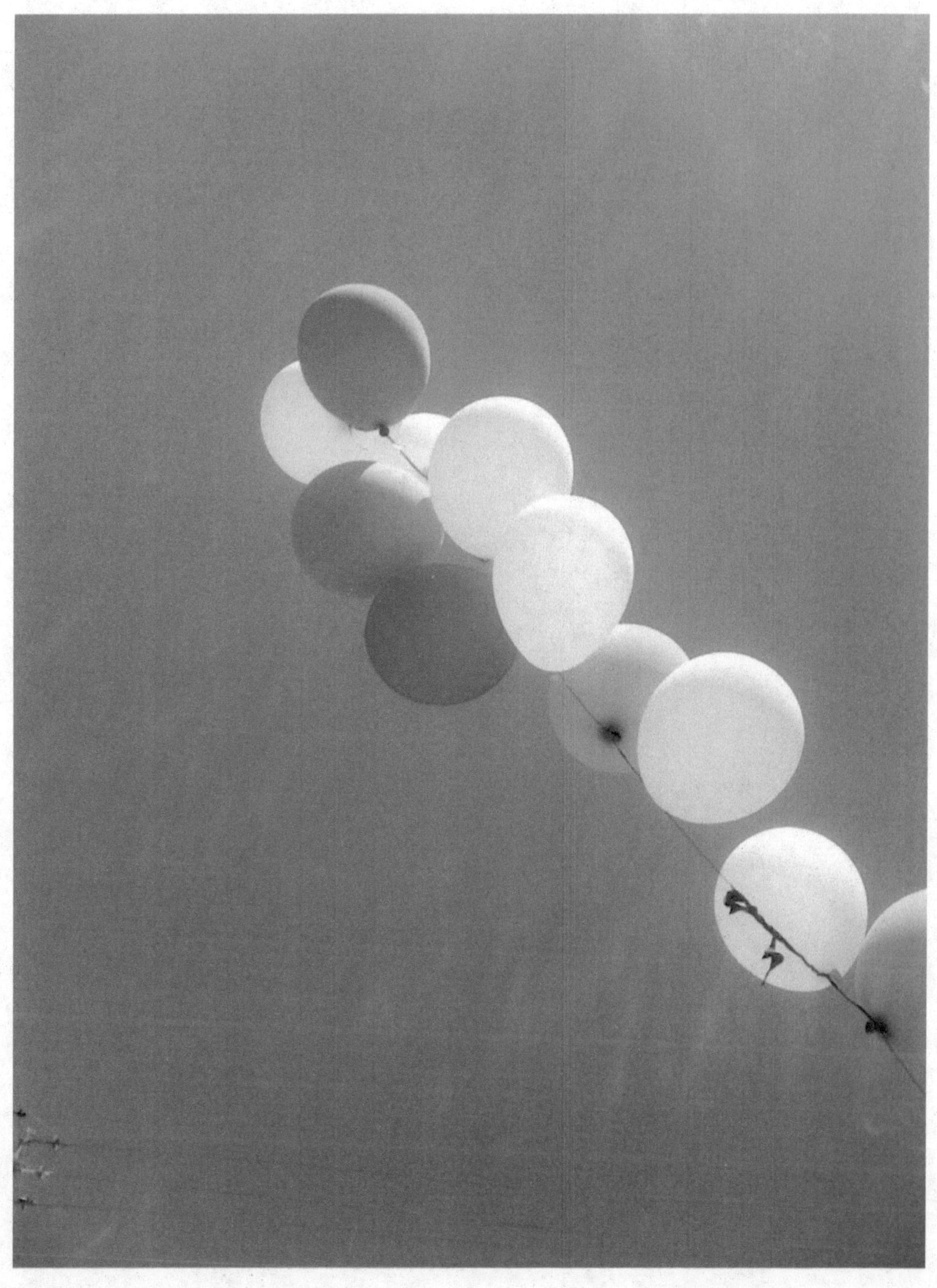

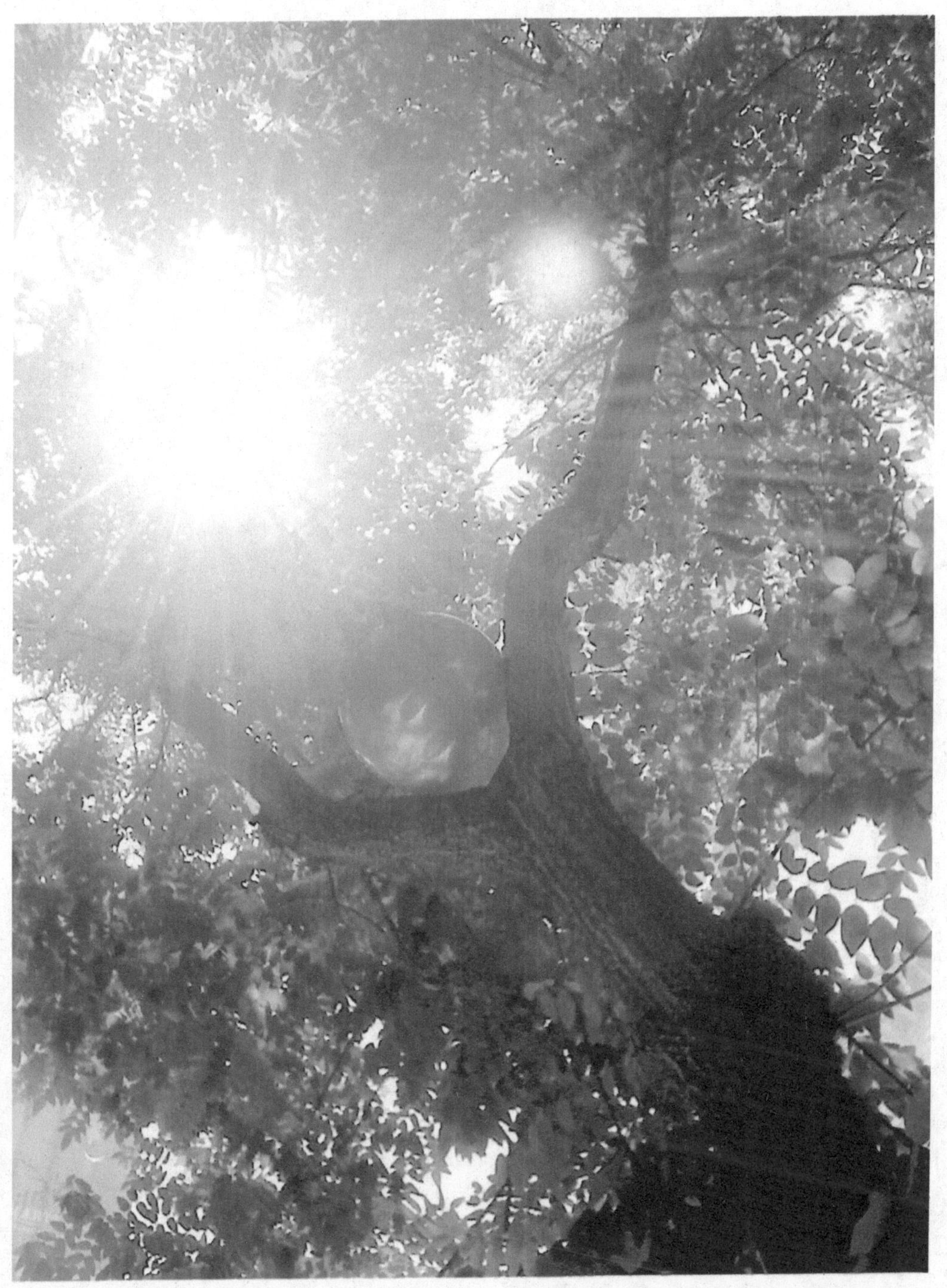

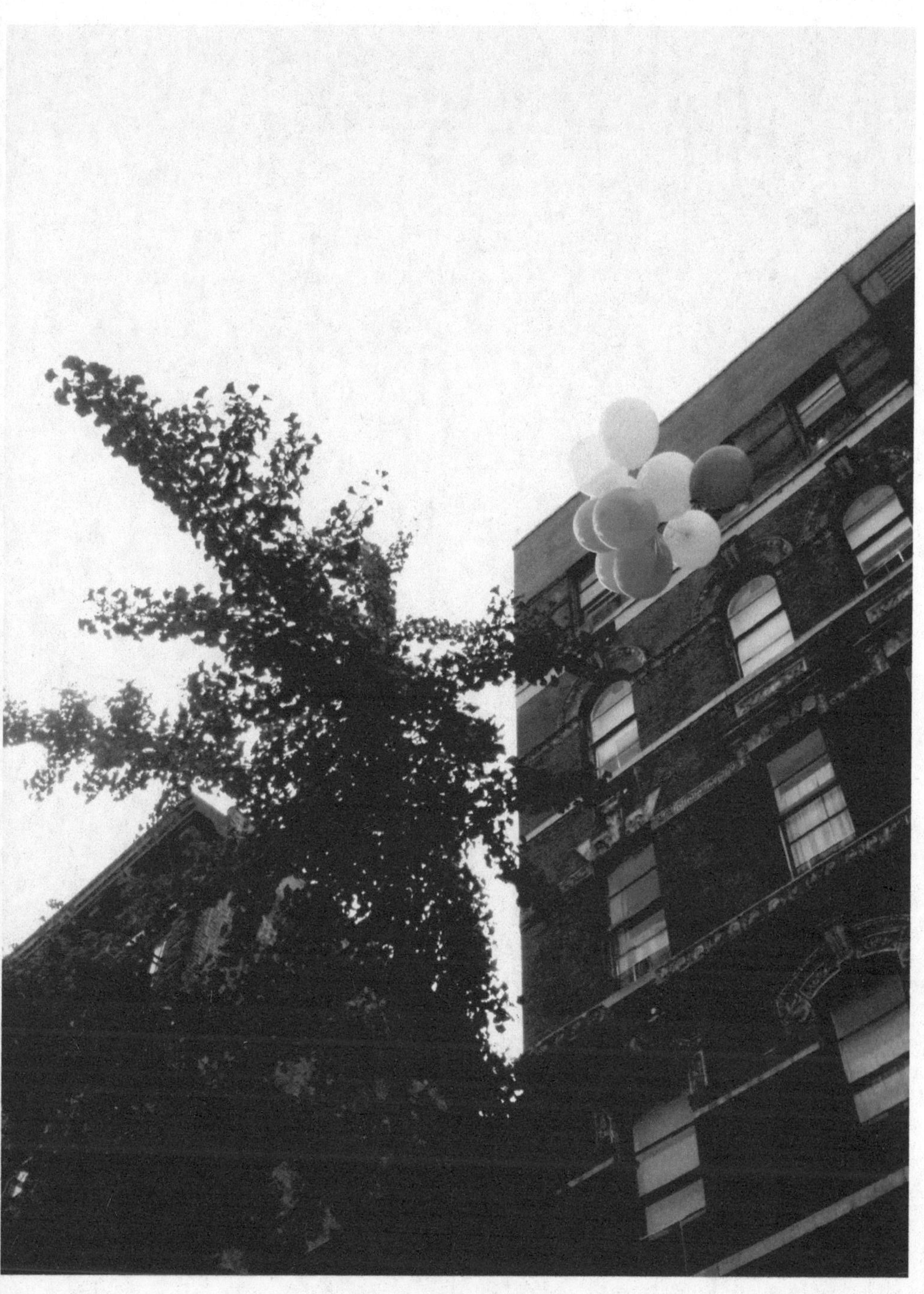

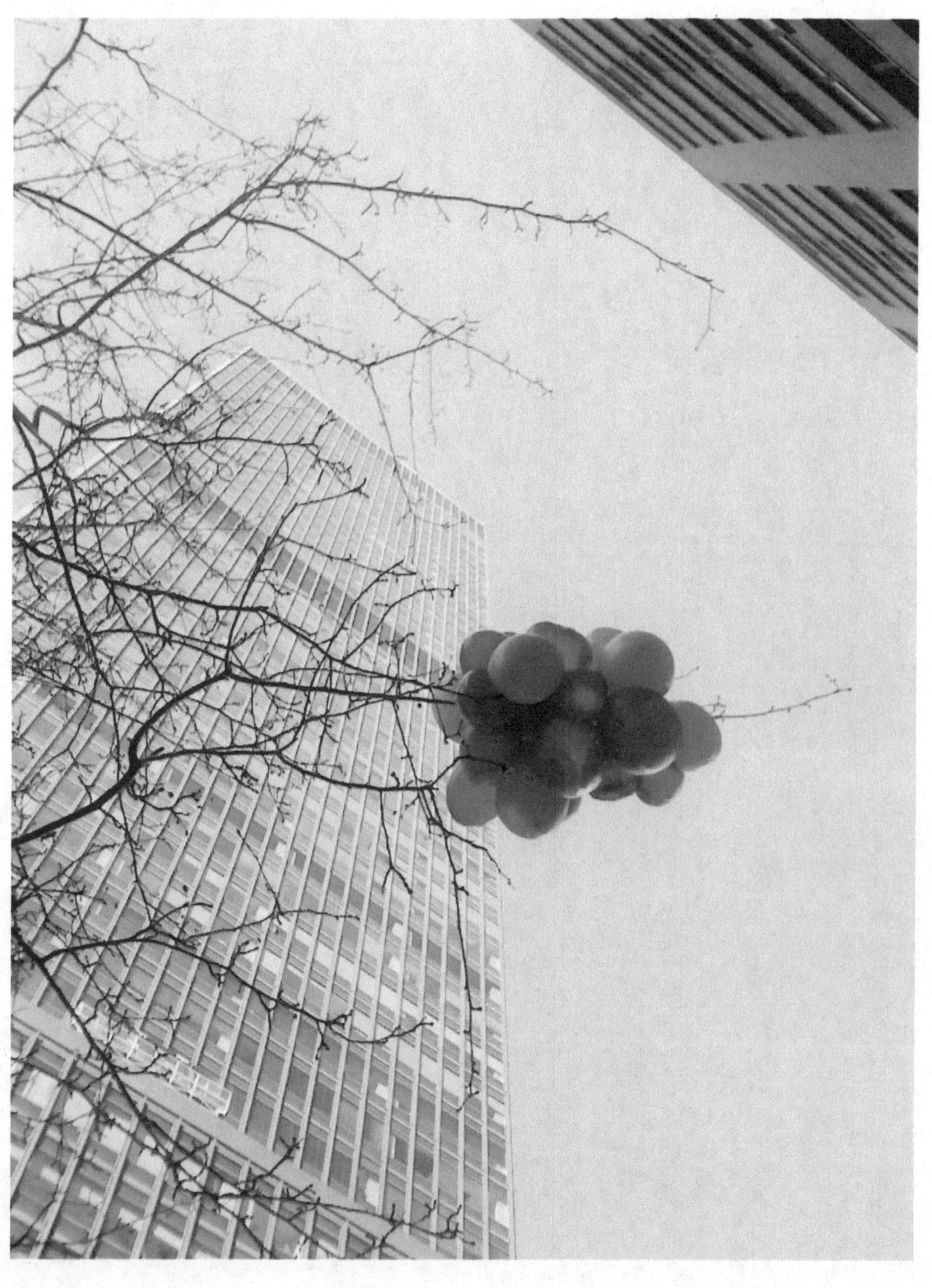

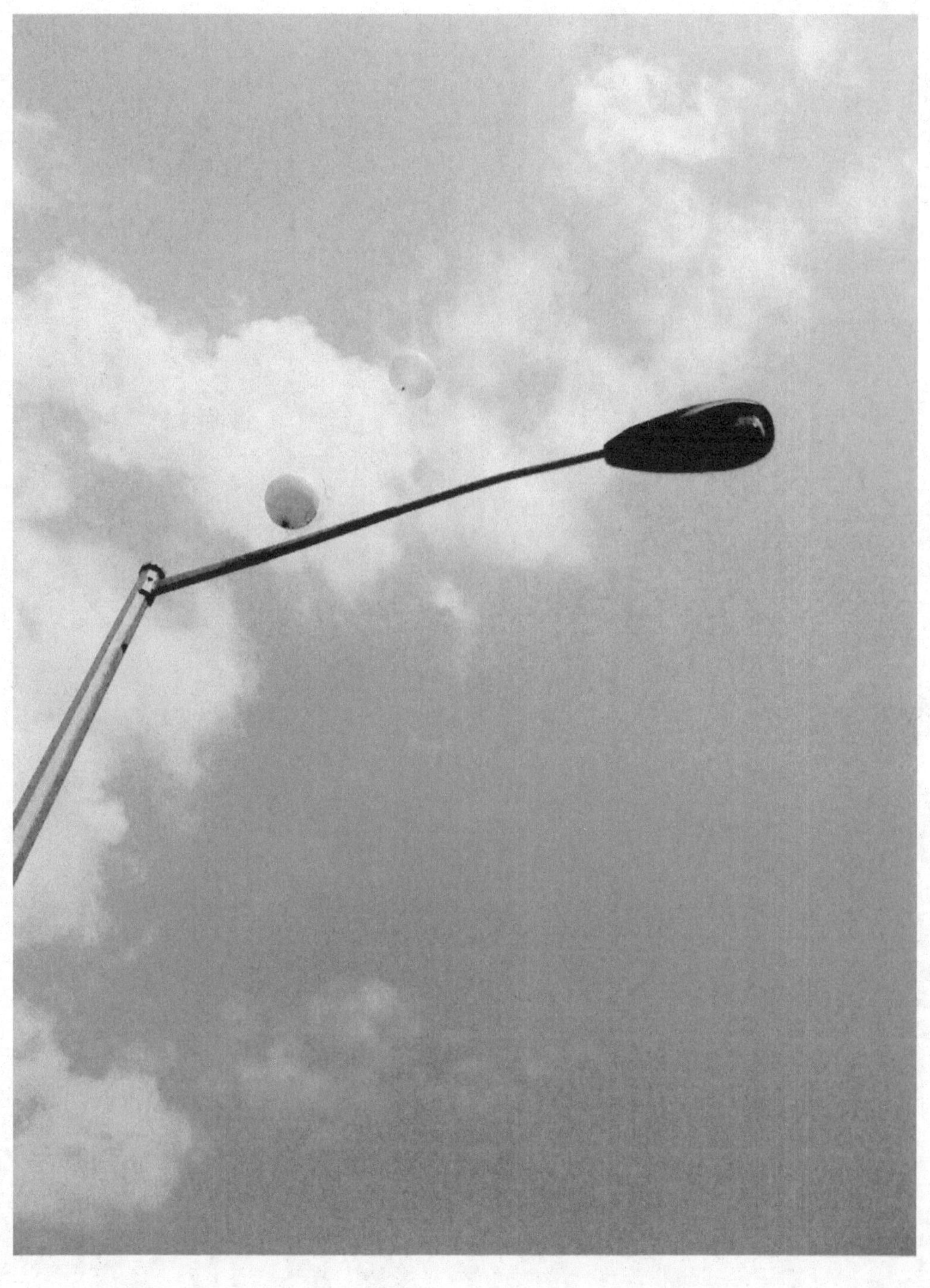

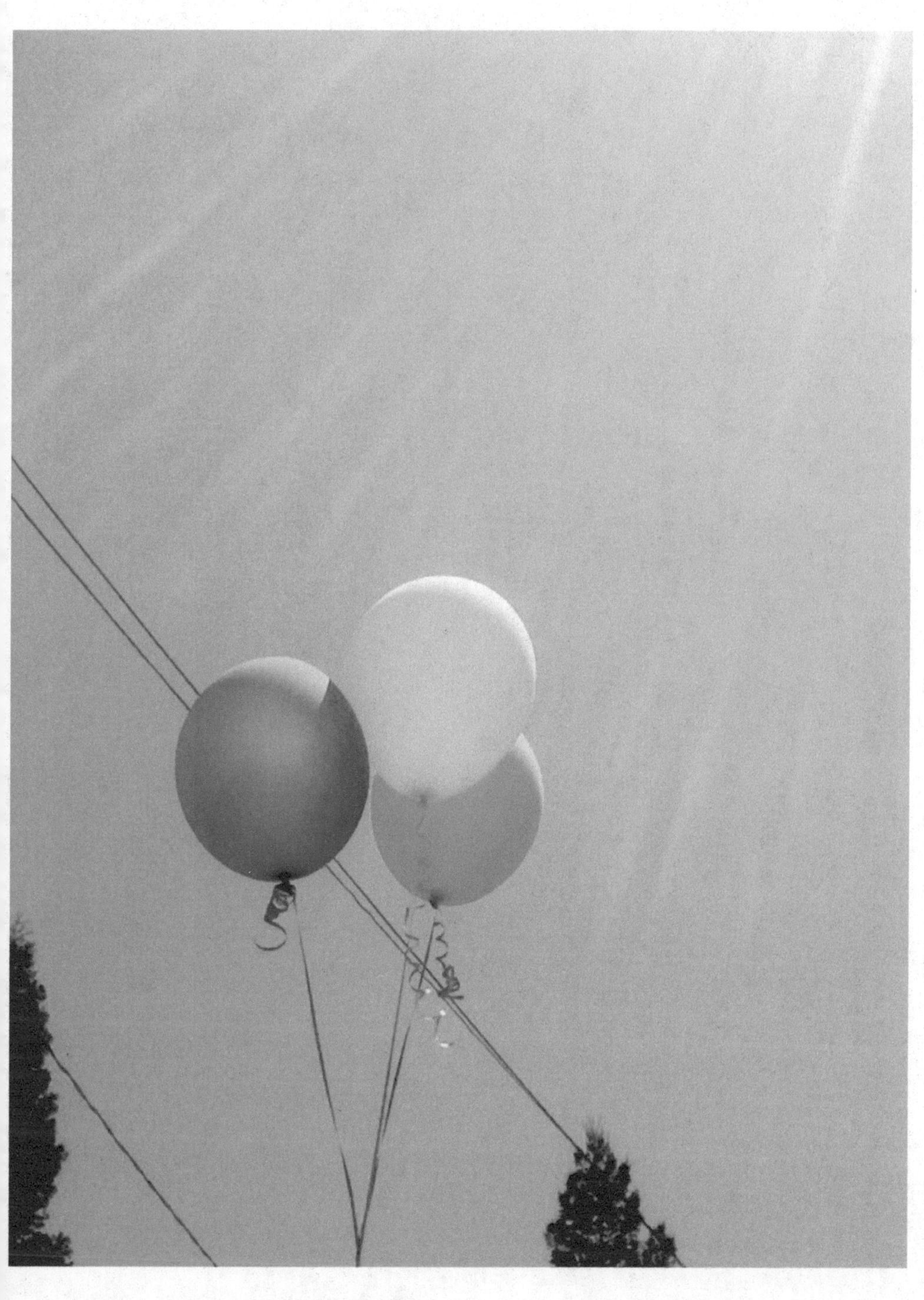

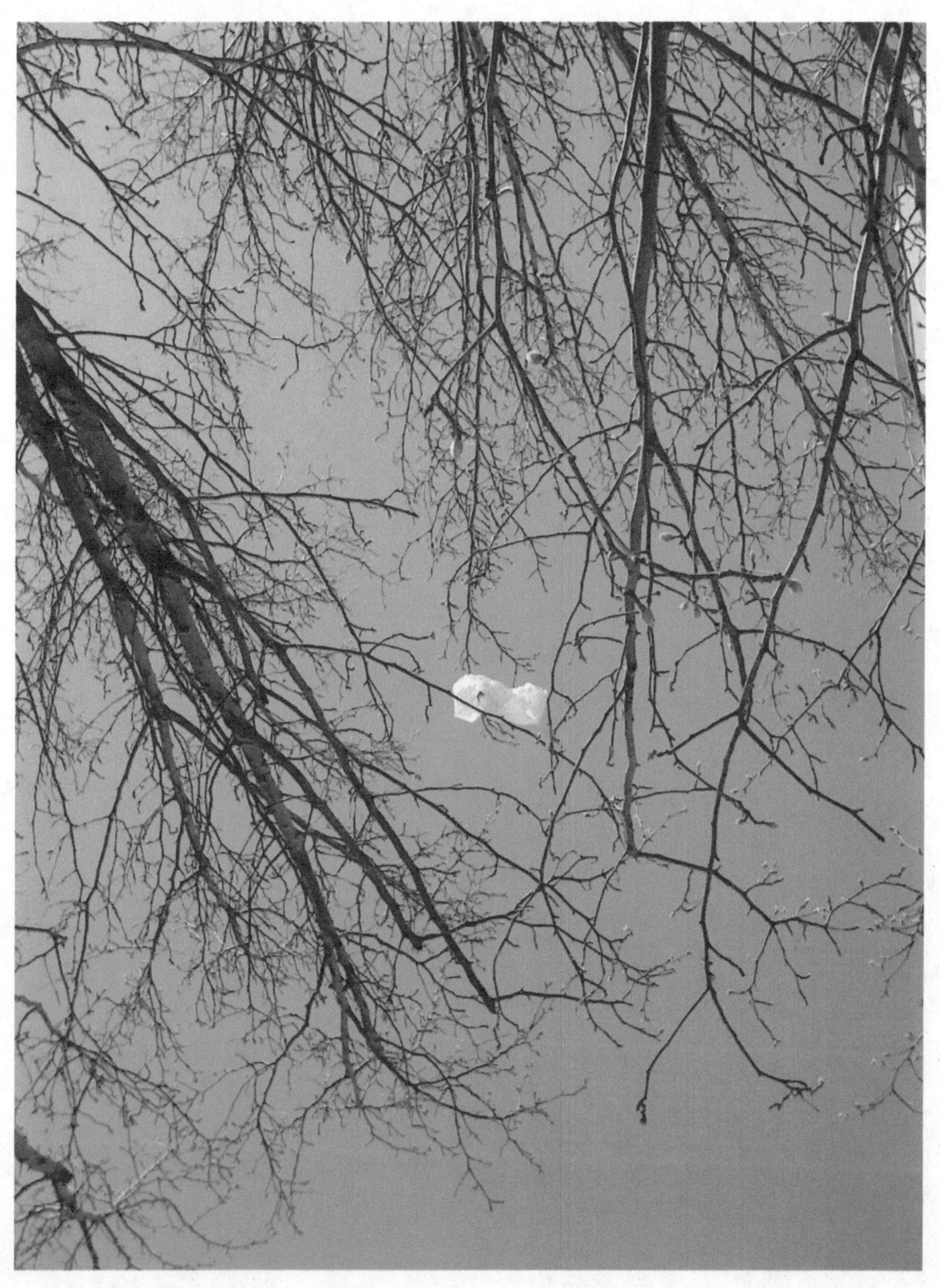

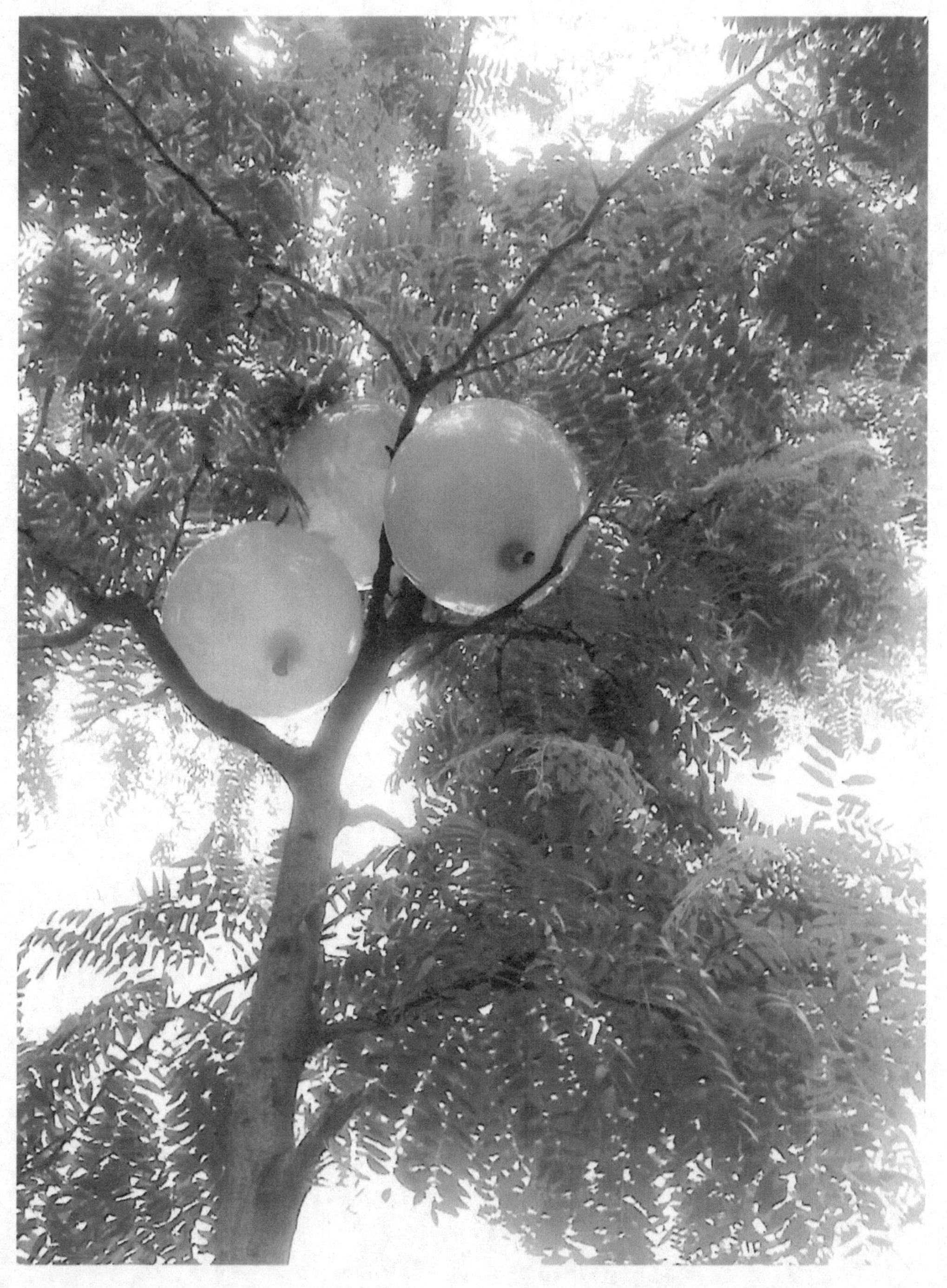

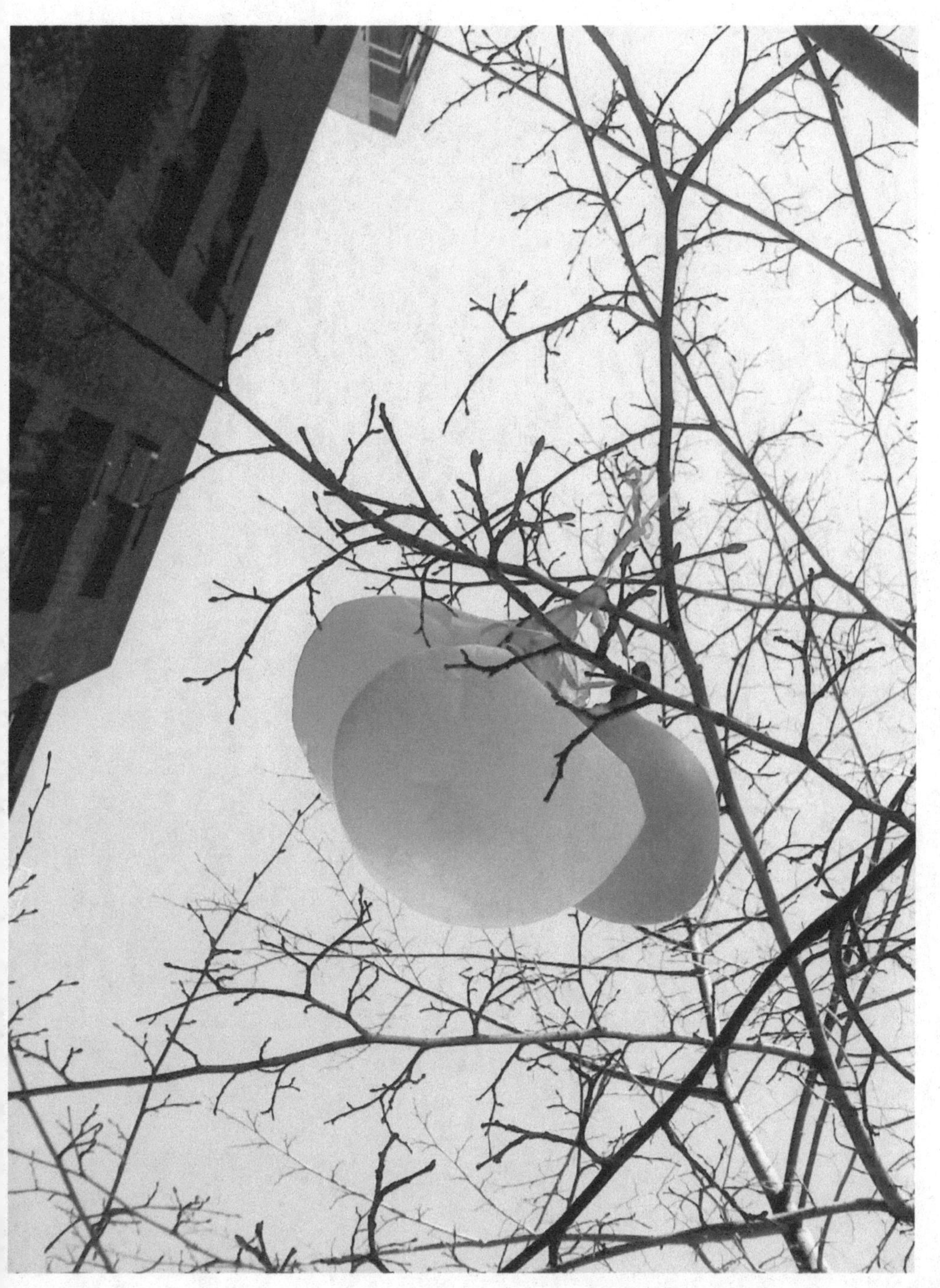

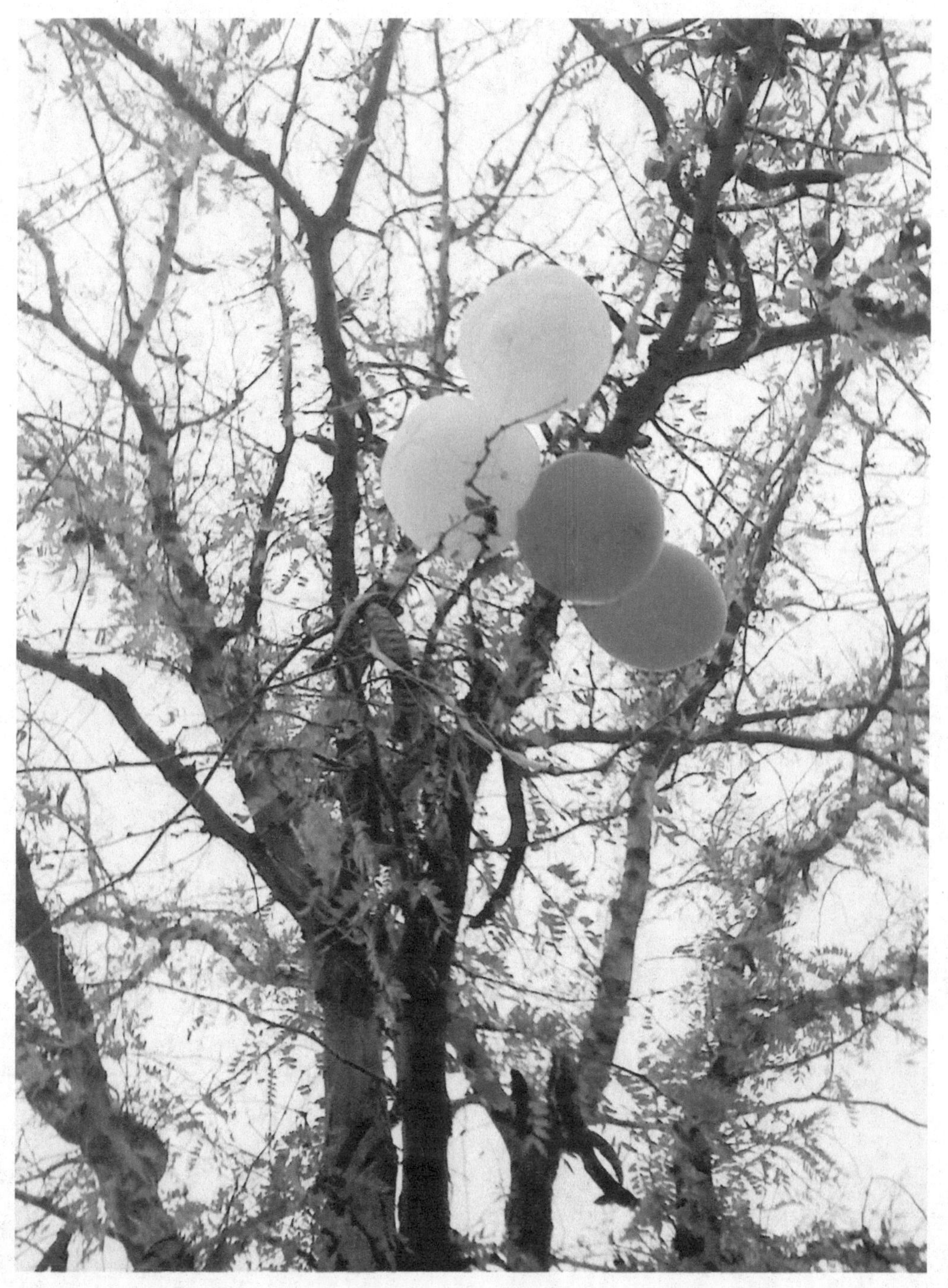

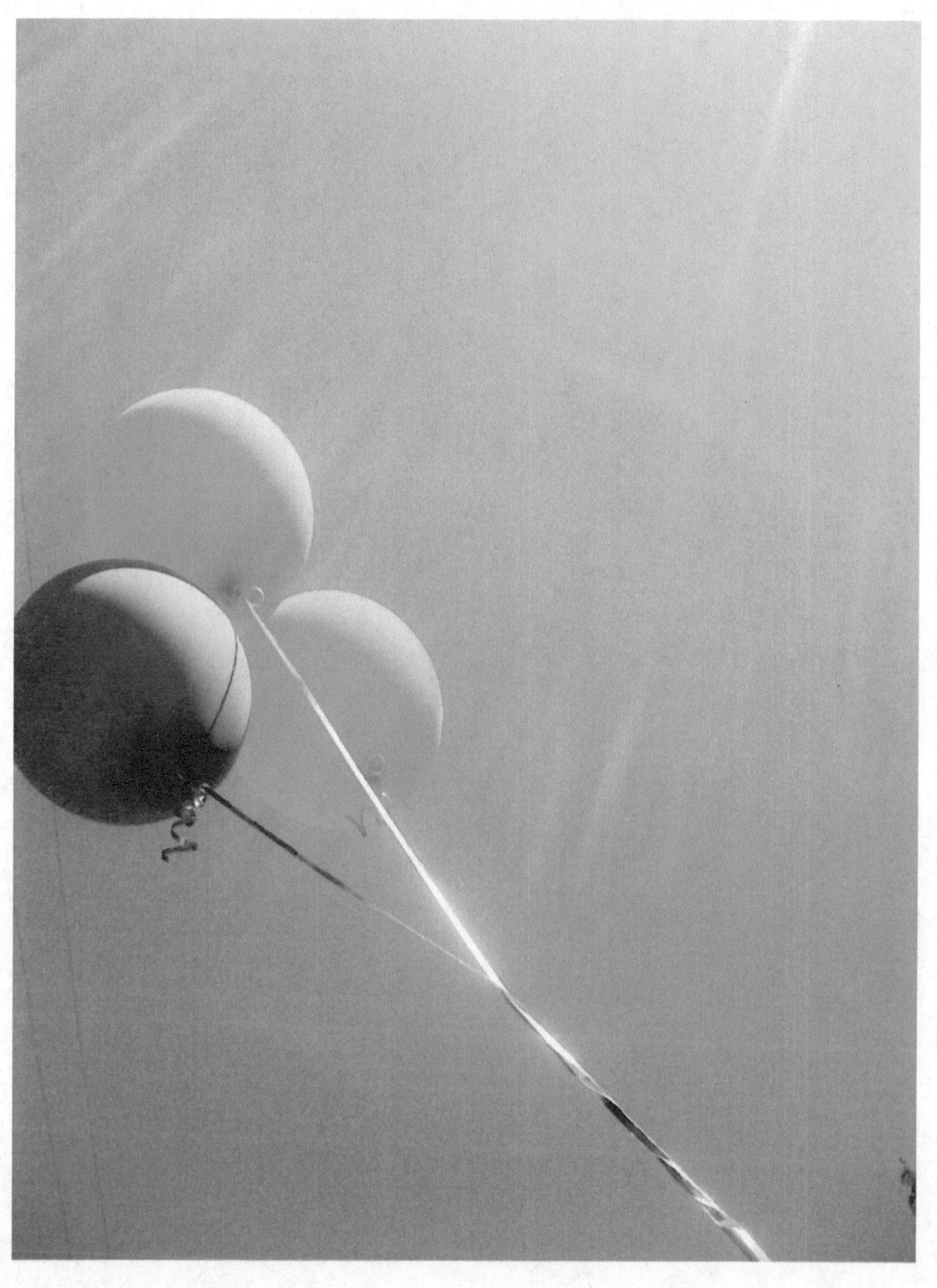

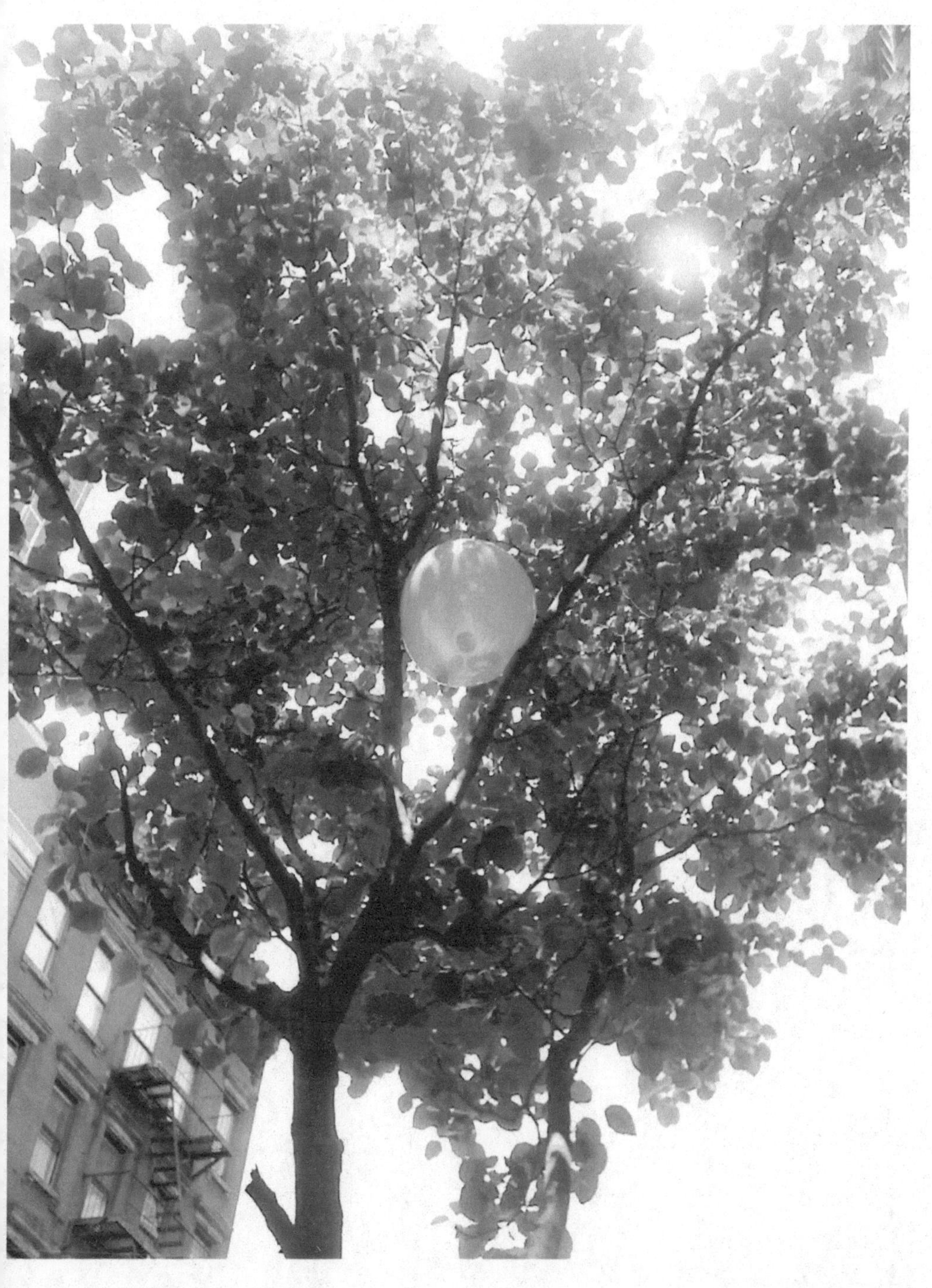

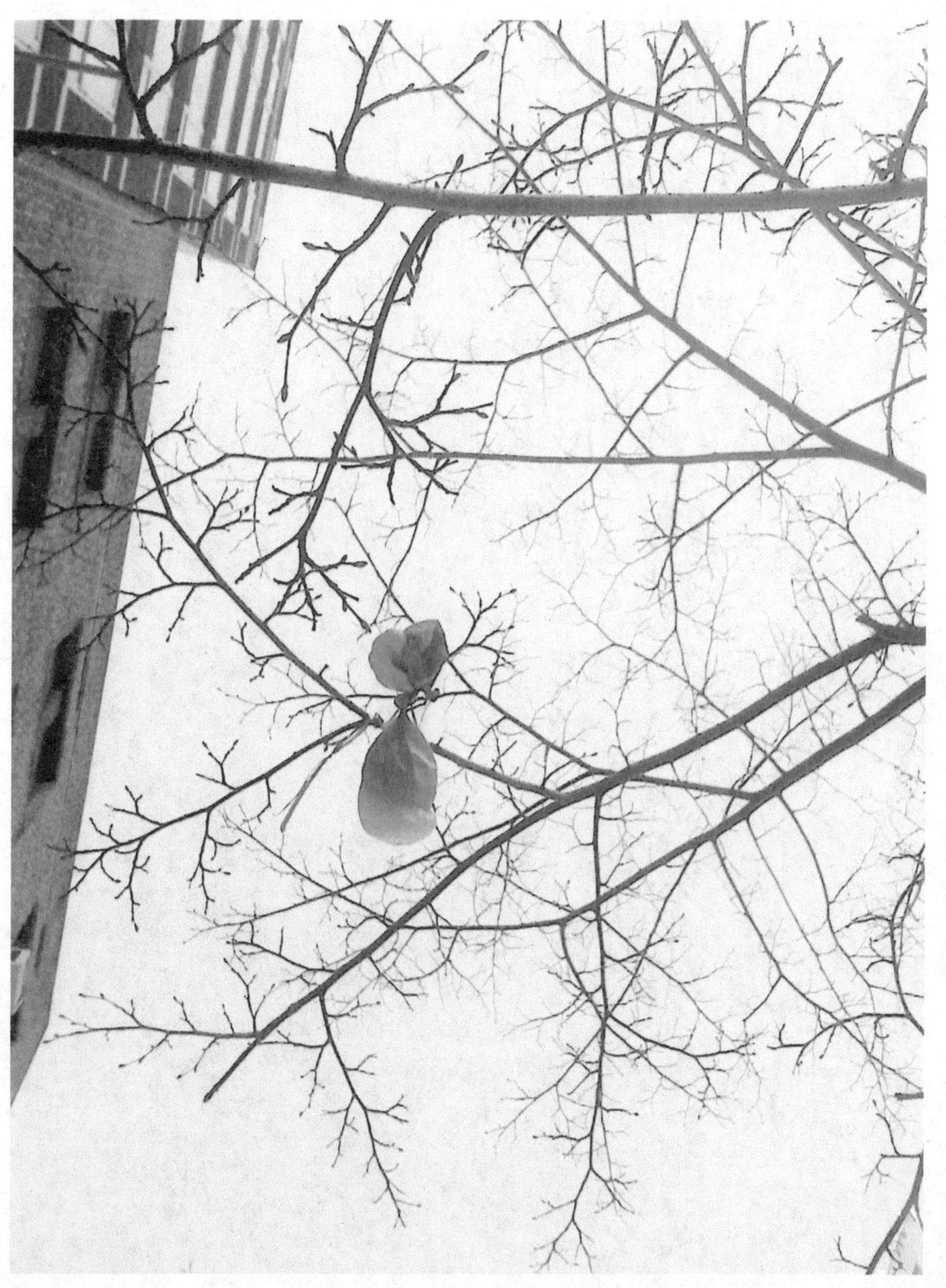

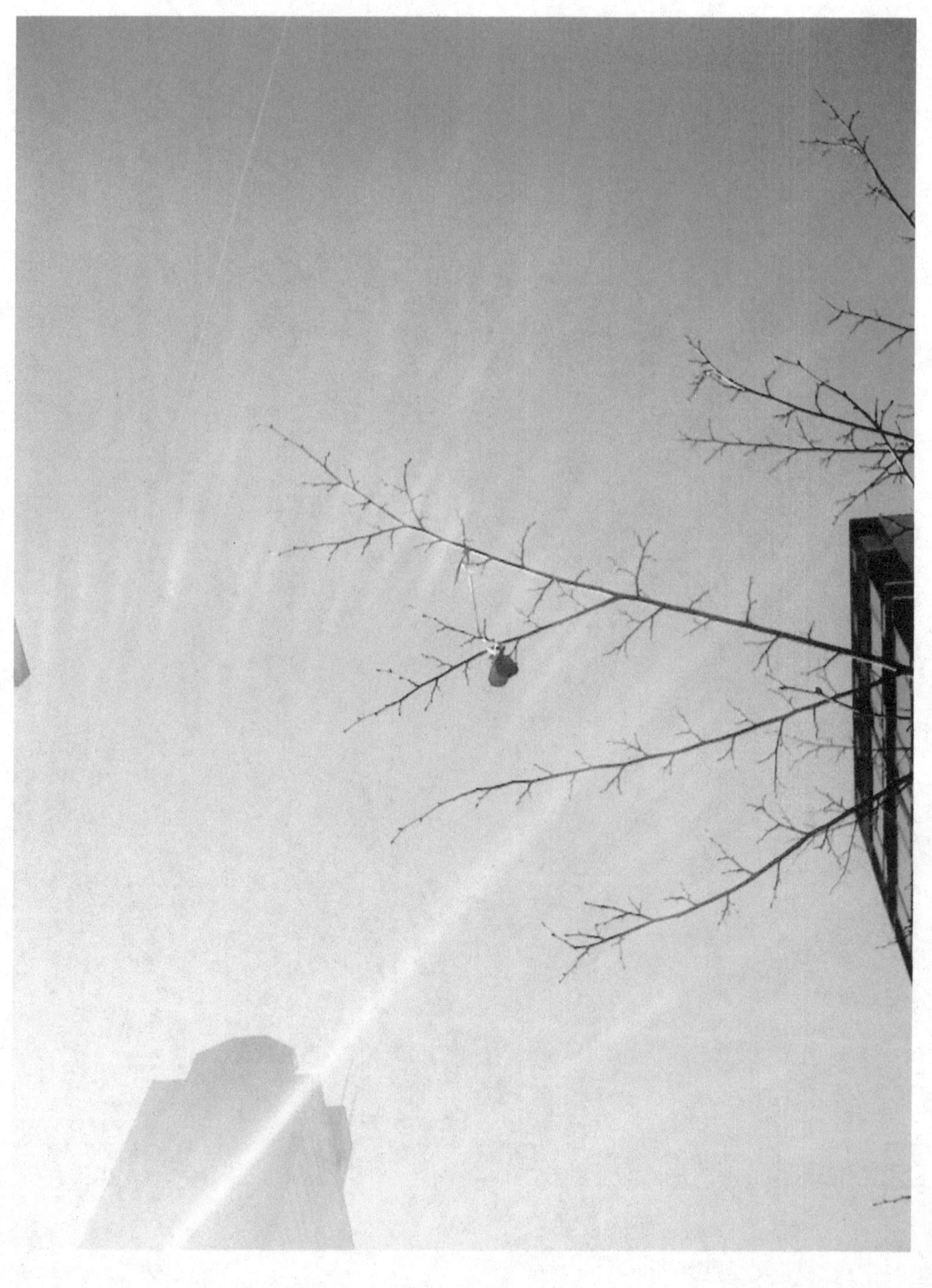

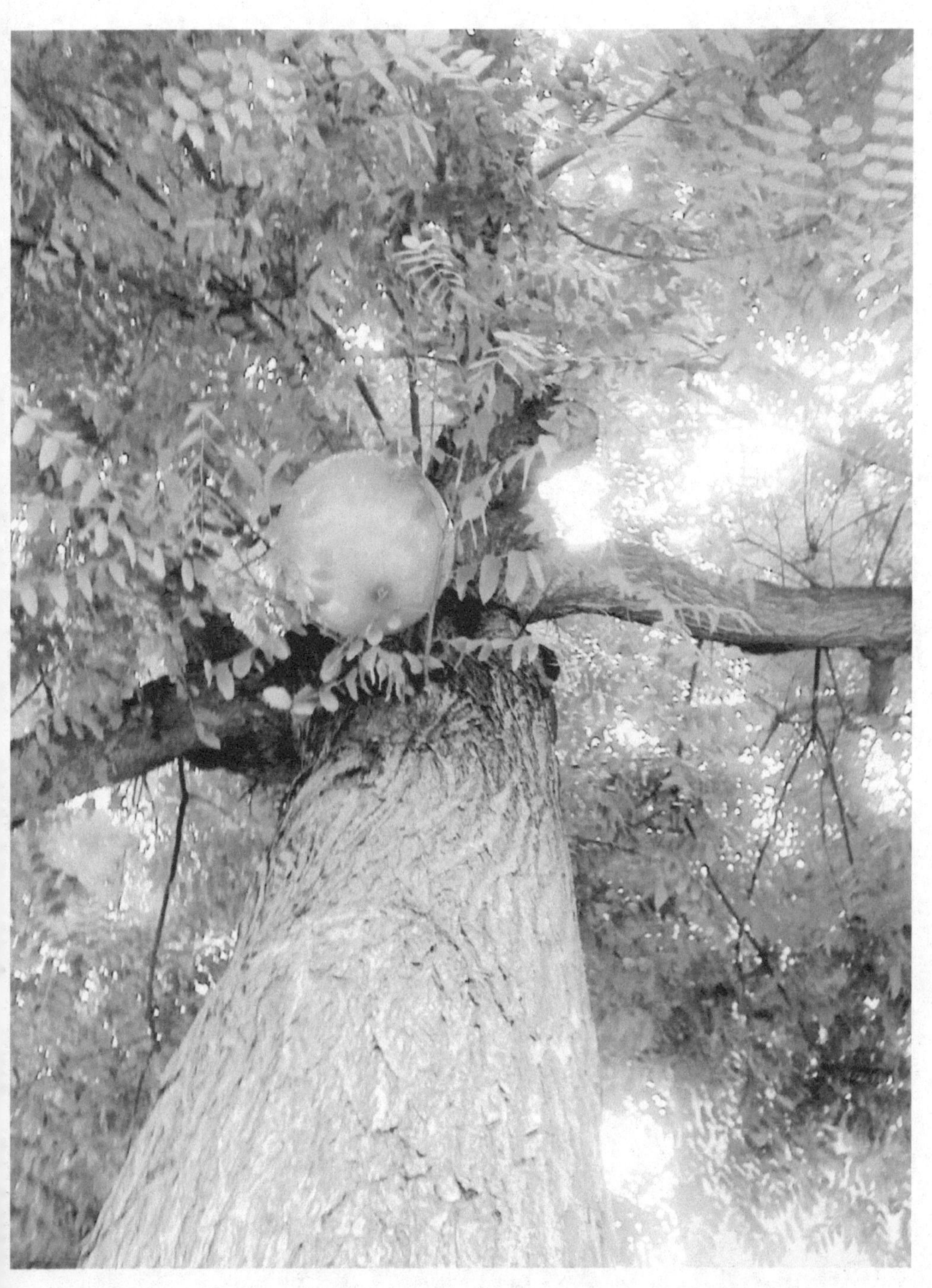

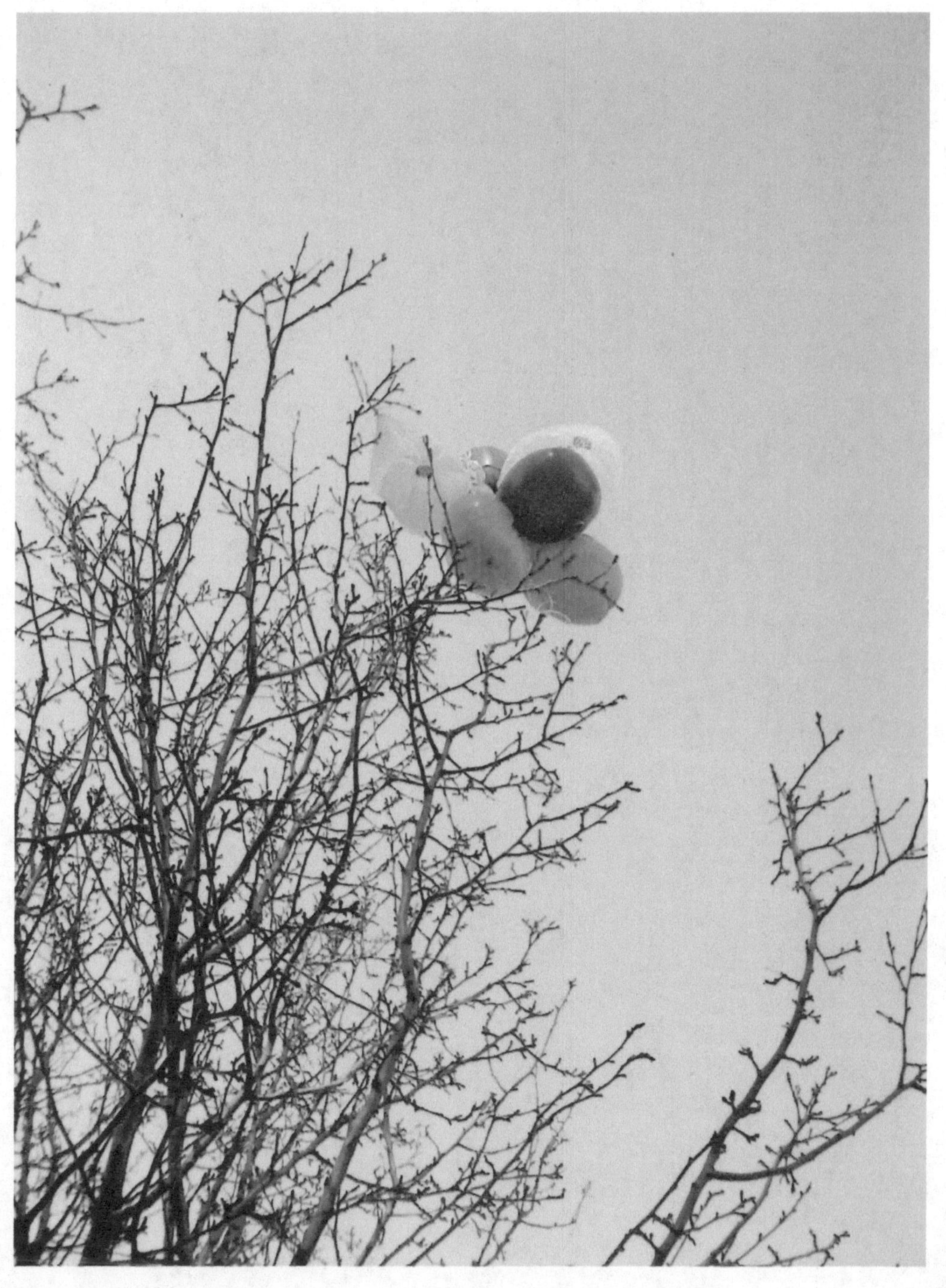

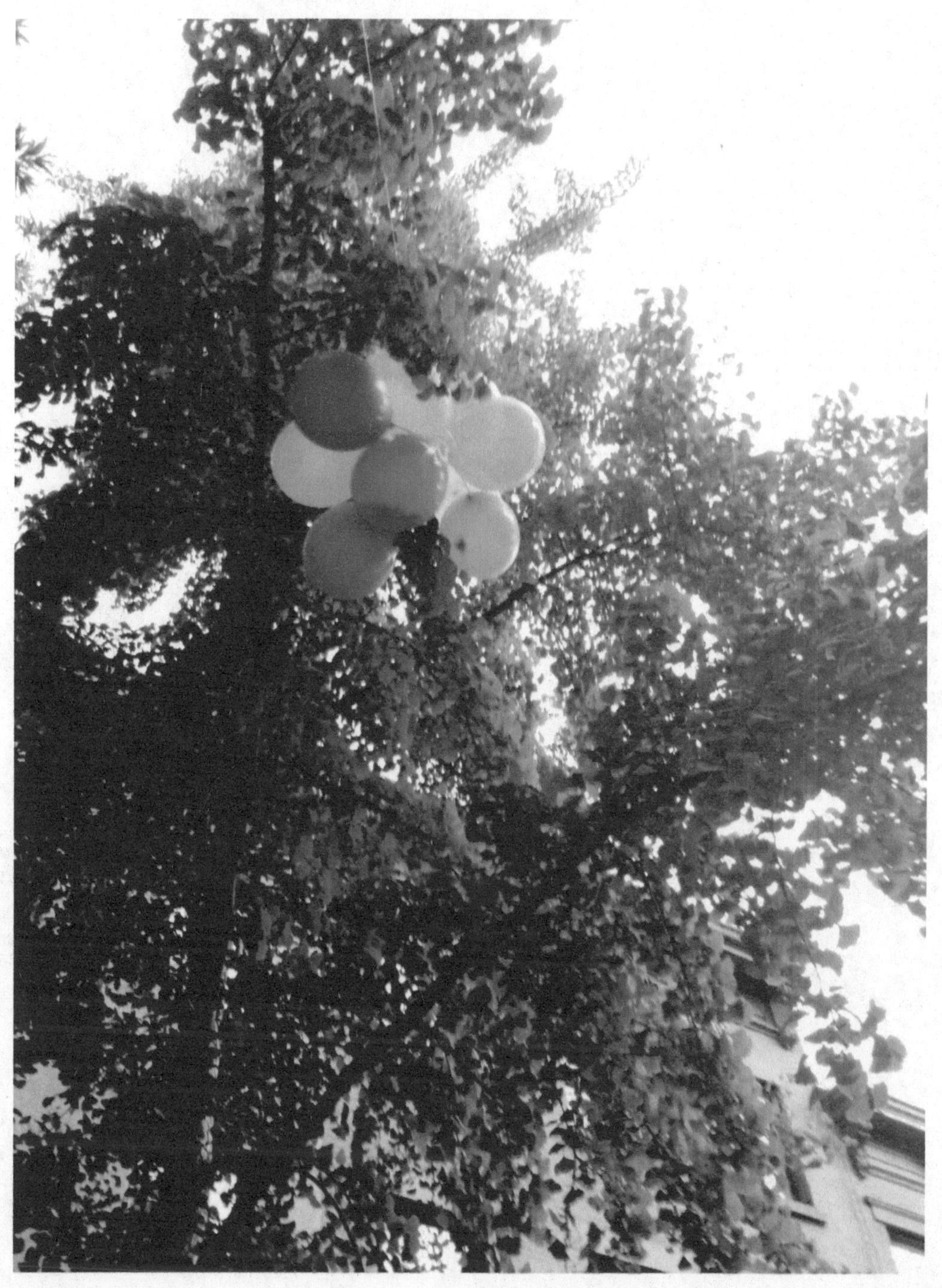

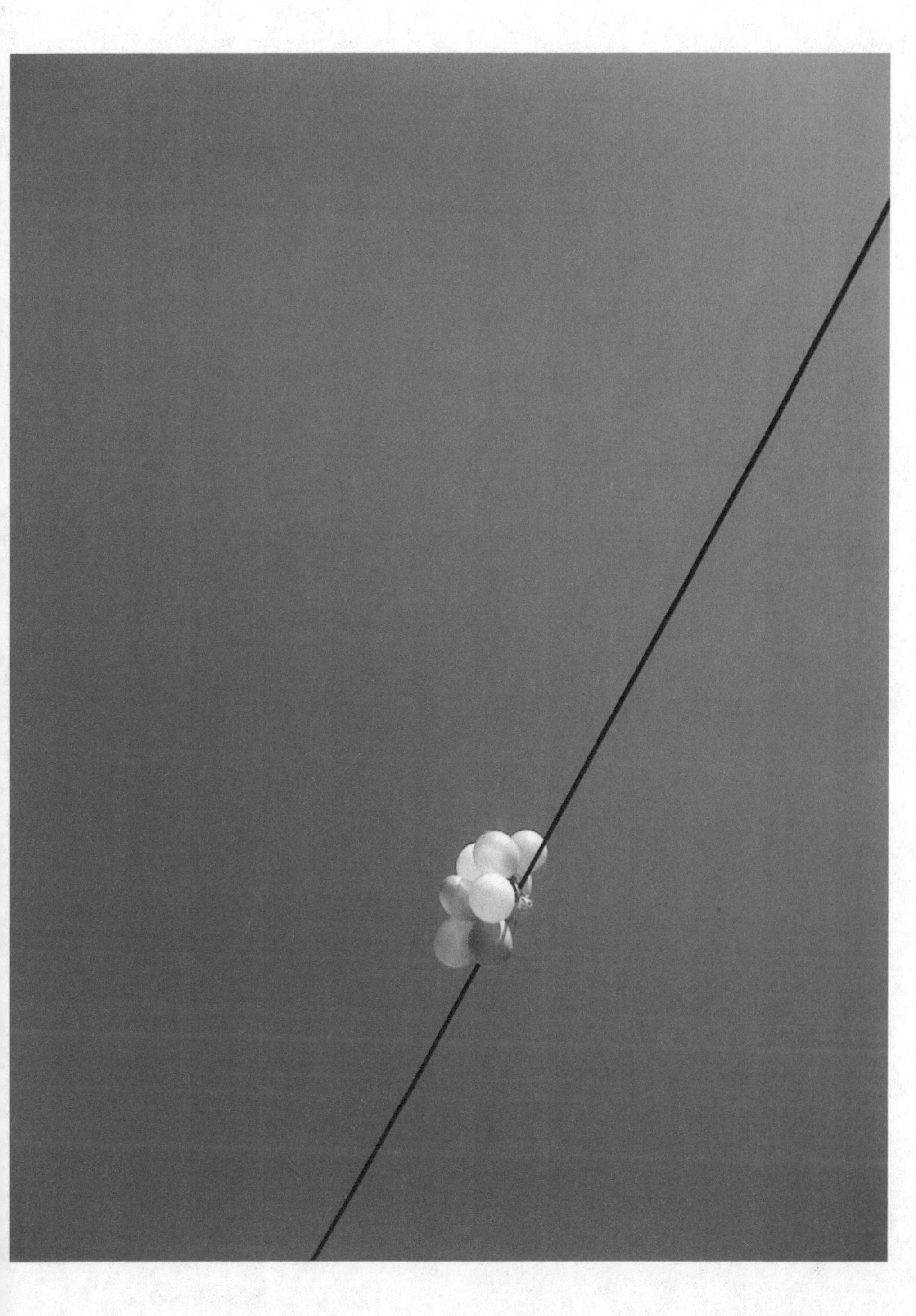

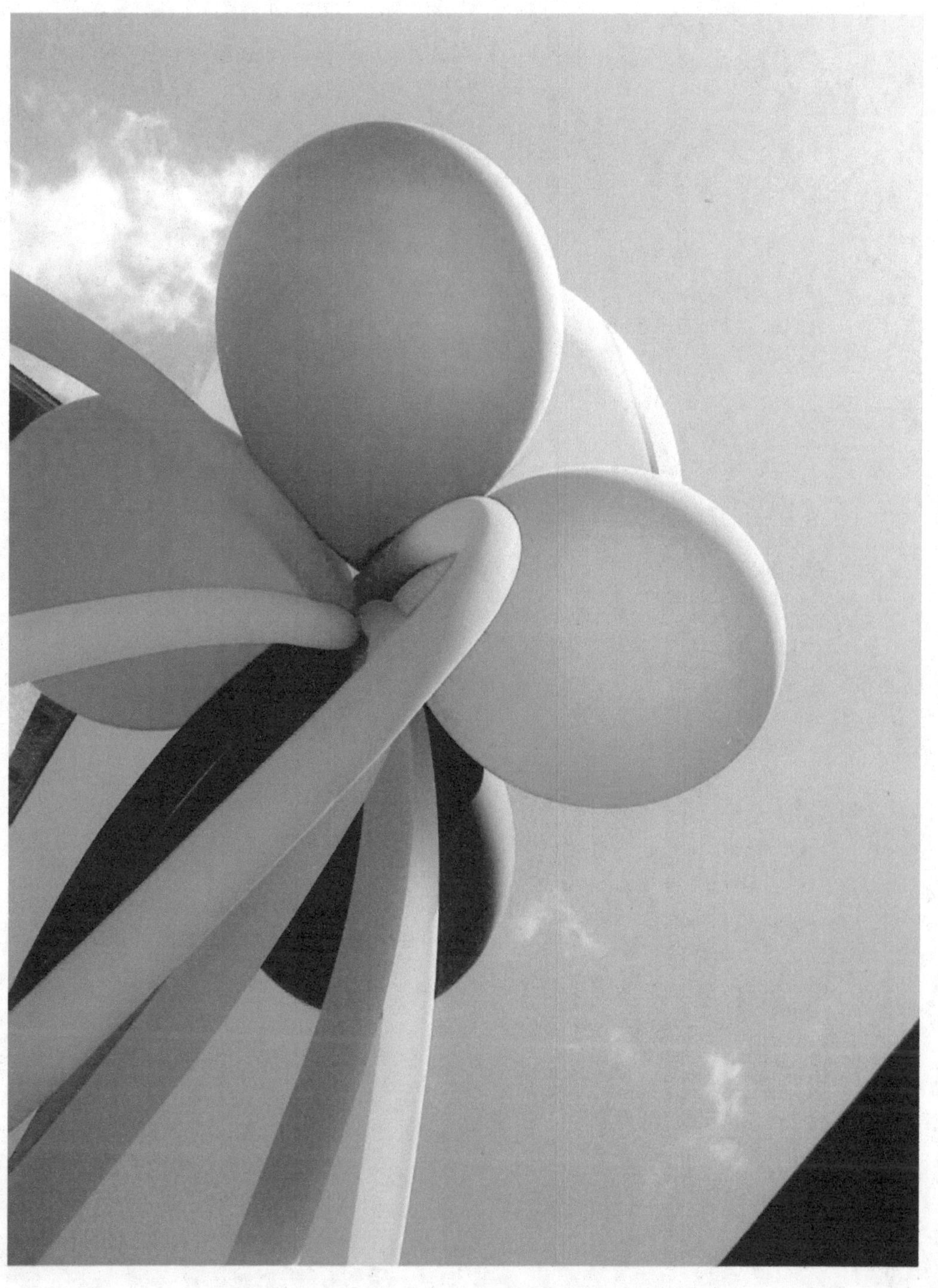

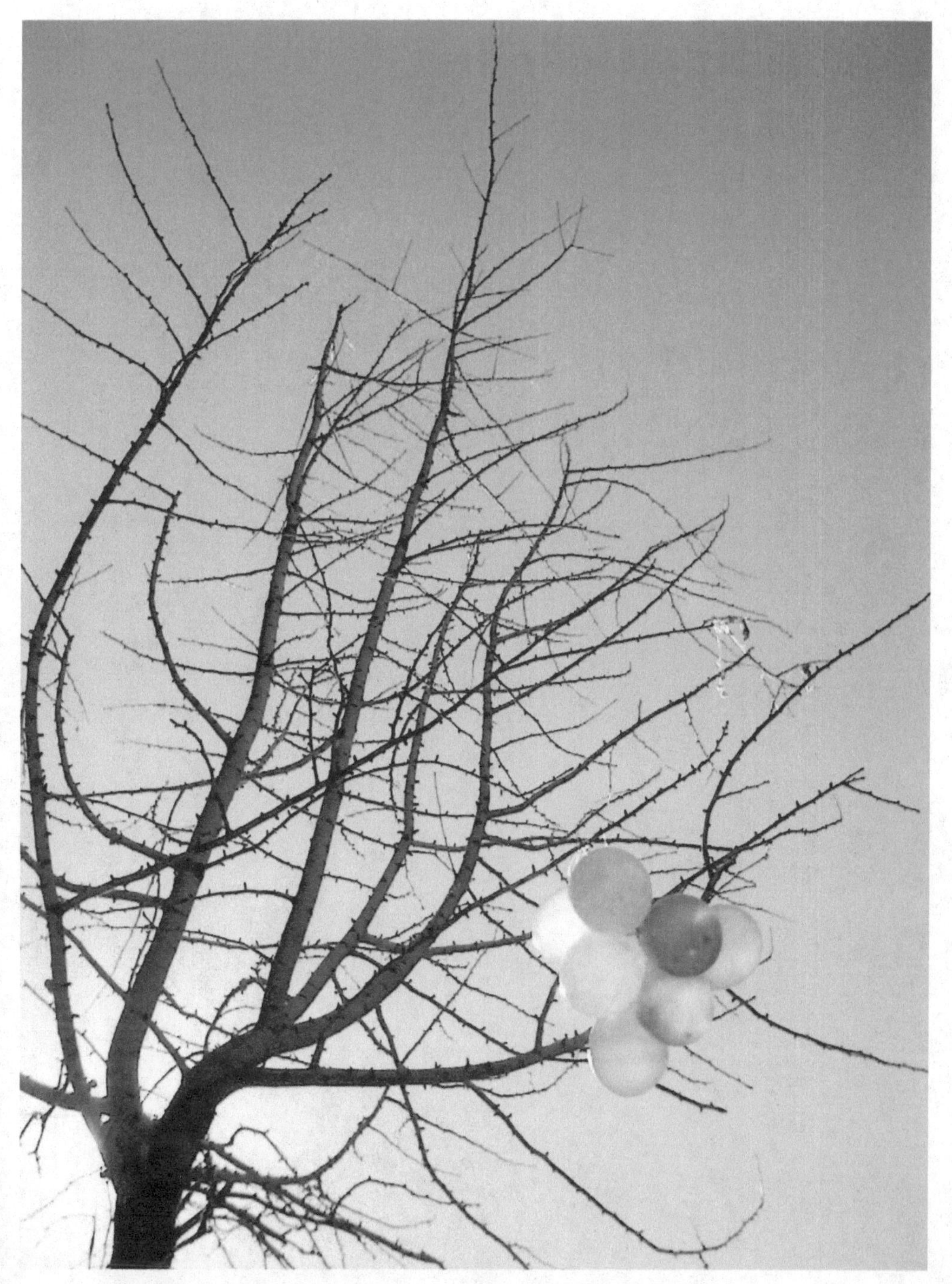

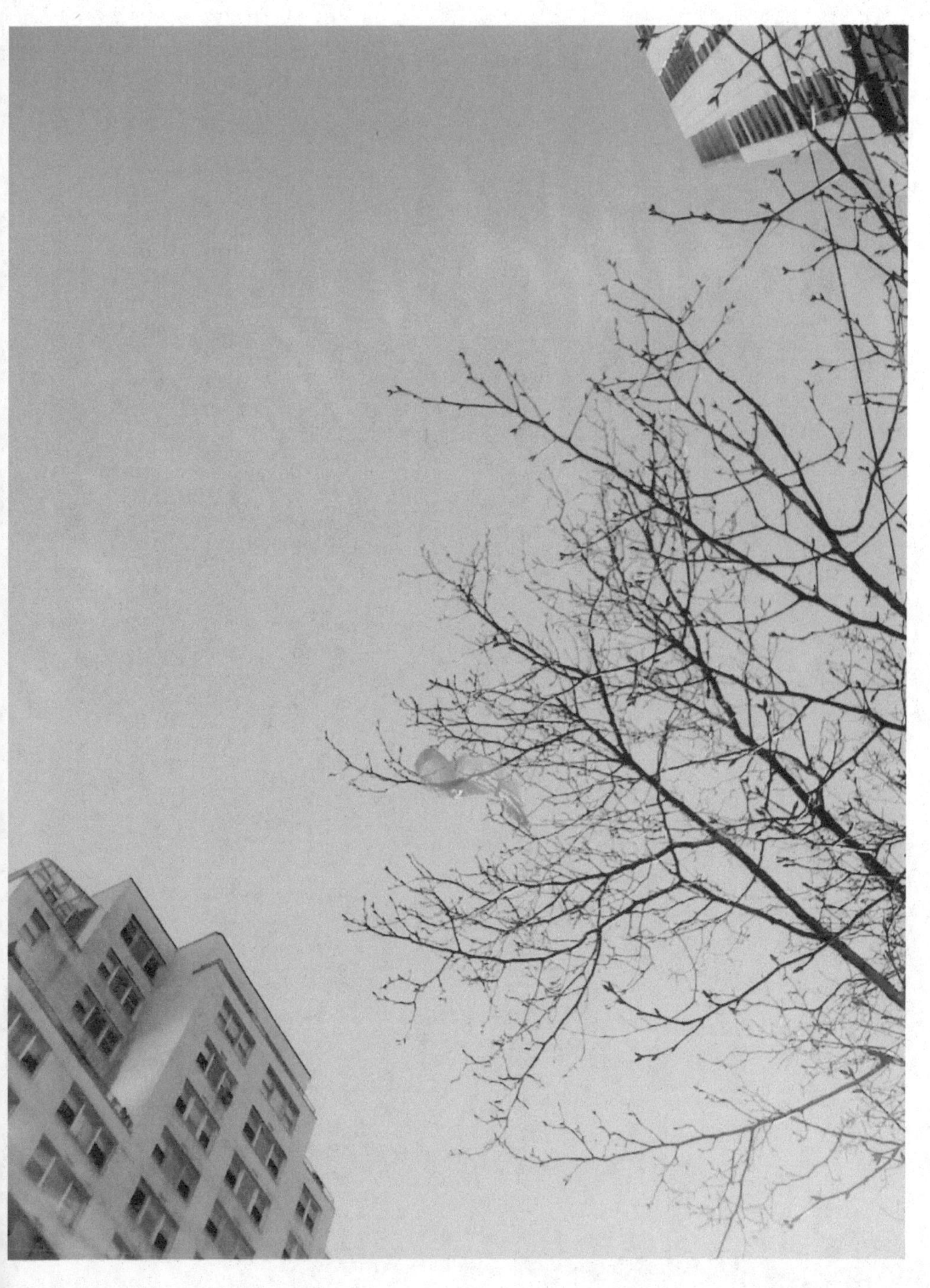

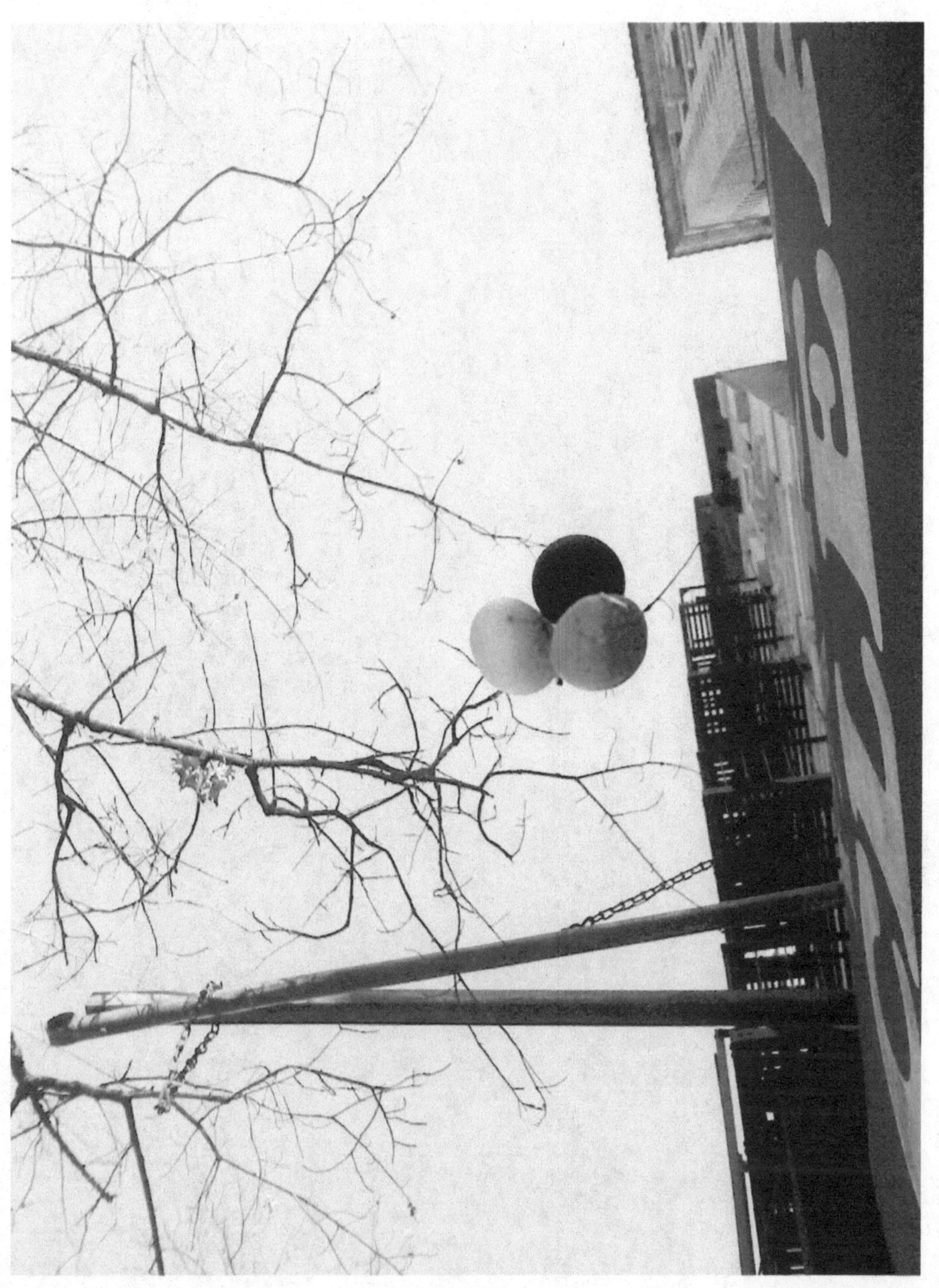

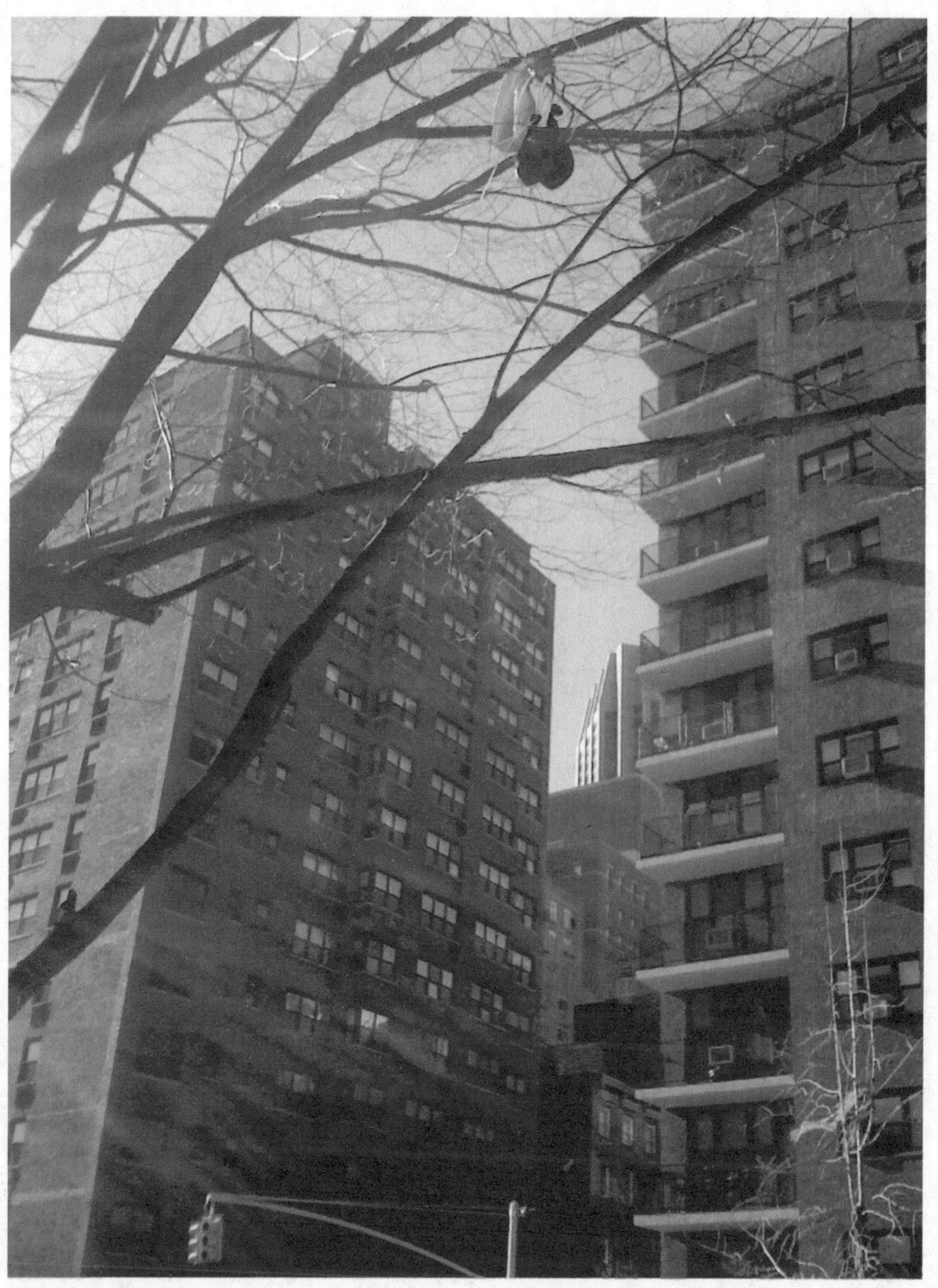

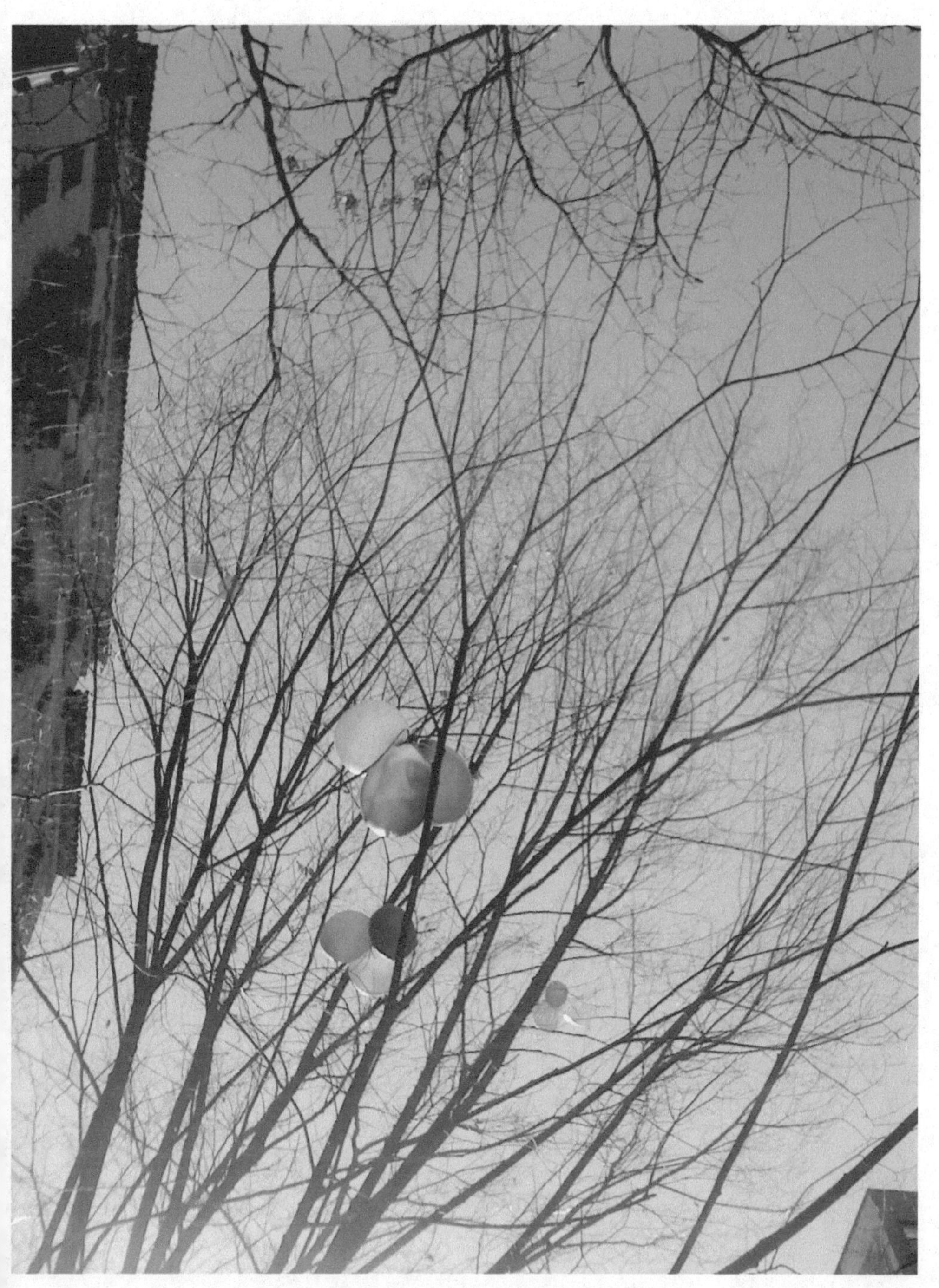

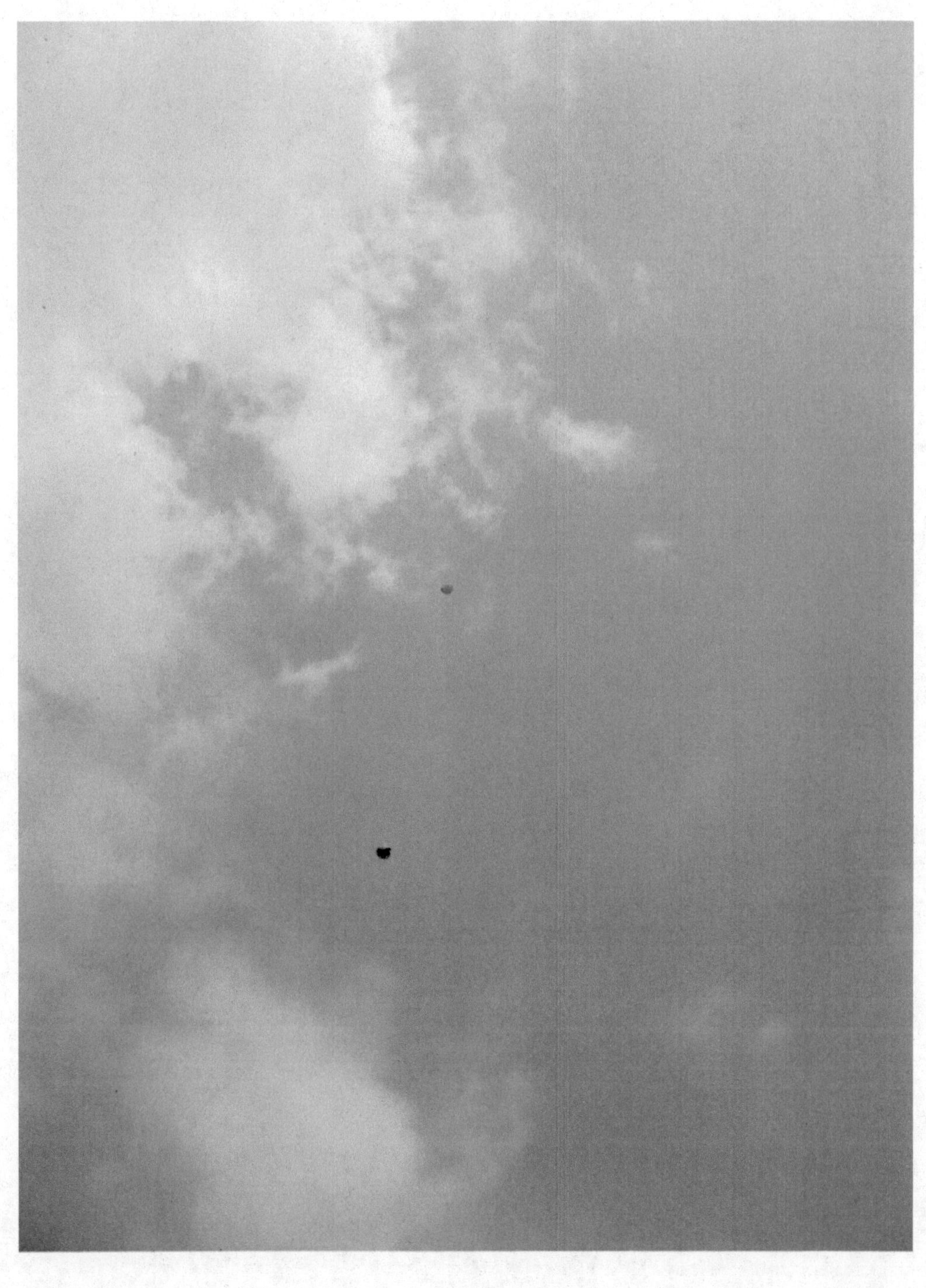

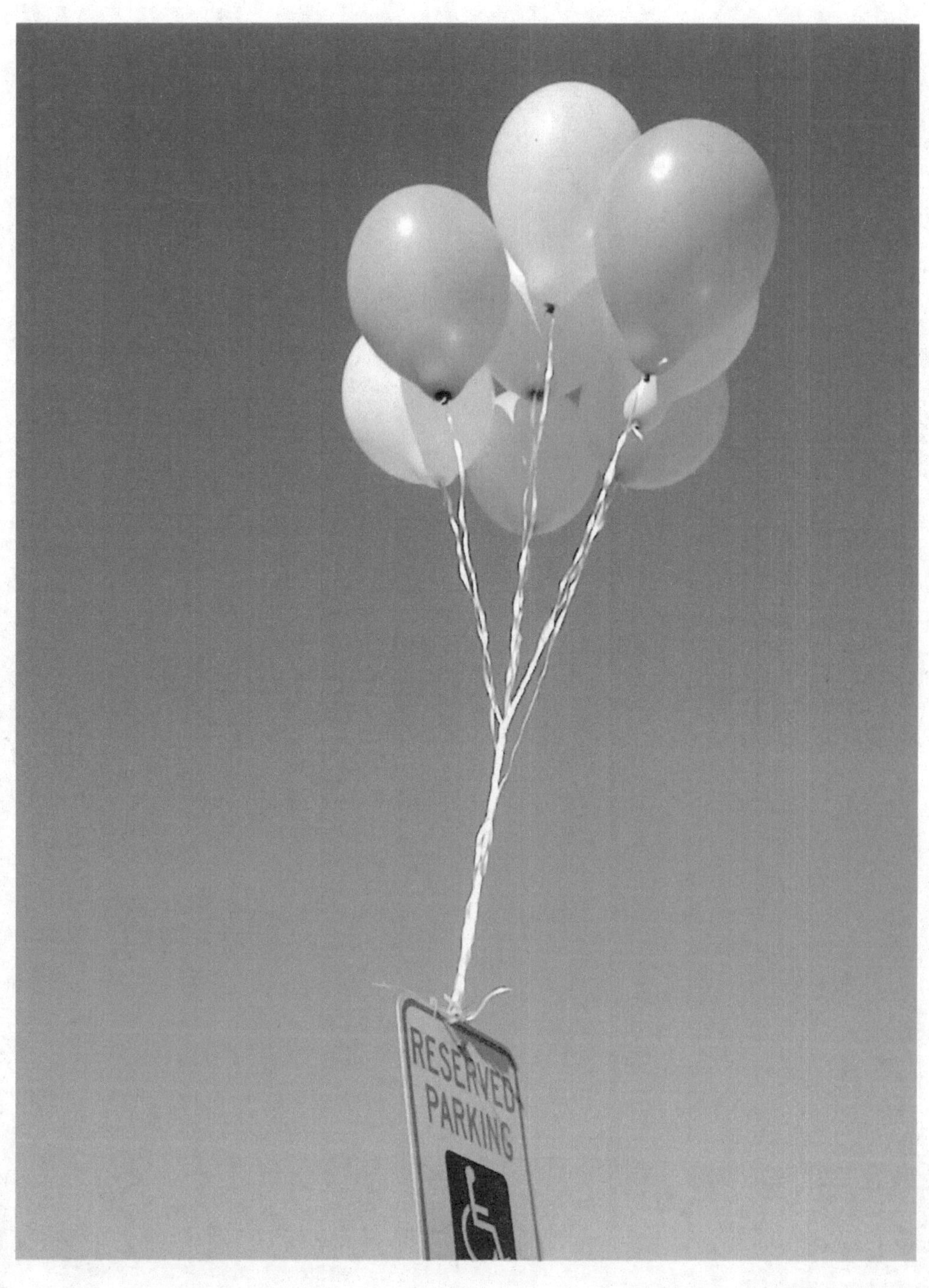
RESERVED
PARKING

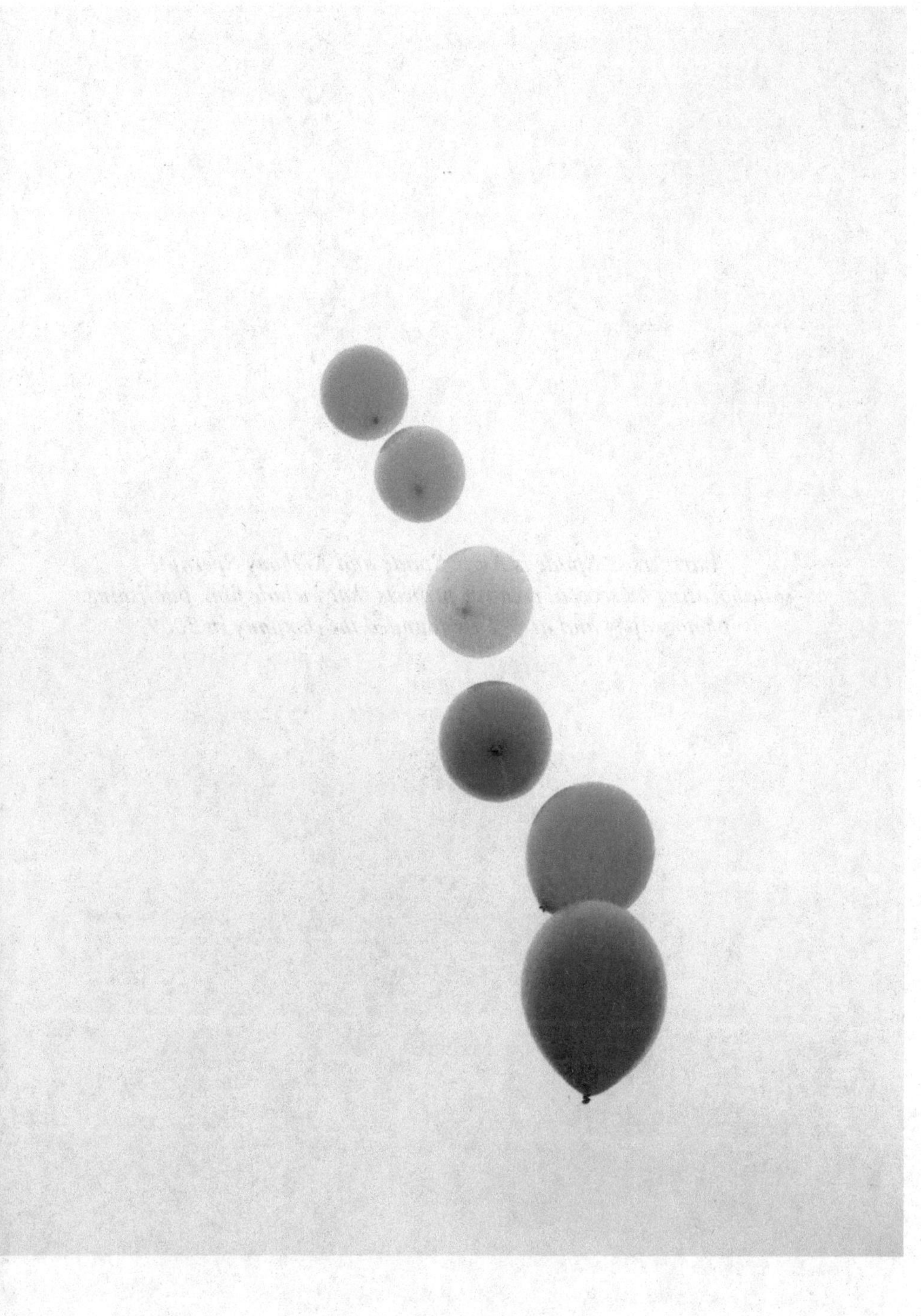

Partners & Spade is Andy Spade and Anthony Sperduti collaborating on several creative projects that include film, publishing, photography and art. They founded the company in 2009.

www.ingramcontent.com/pod-product-compliance
Lightning Source LLC
La Vergne TN
LVHW030922080826
845145LV00013B/3023

* 9 7 8 0 0 6 1 9 0 1 6 6 9 *